Lidia's a Pot, a Pan, and a Bowl

Felidia

My American Dream

Lidia's Celebrate Like an Italian

Lidia's Mastering the Art of Italian Cuisine

Lidia's Egg-citing Farm Adventure

Lidia's Commonsense Italian Cooking

Lidia's Family Kitchen: Nonna's Birthday Surprise

Lidia's Favorite Recipes

Lidia's Italy in America

Nonna Tell Me a Story: Lidia's Christmas Kitchen

Lidia Cooks from the Heart of Italy

Lidia's Italy

Lidia's Family Table

Lidia's Italian-American Kitchen

Lidia's Italian Table

La Cucina di Lidia

— LIDIA'S FROM OUR —

FAMILY TABLE

— TO YOURS —

—— LIDIA'S FROM OUR ——

FAMILY TABLE

—— TO YOURS ——

More Than 100 Recipes Made with Love for All Occasions

Lidia Matticchio Bastianich and Tanya Bastianich Manuali

Photographs by Armando Rafael

ALFRED A. KNOPF   NEW YORK   2023

THIS IS A BORZOI BOOK
PUBLISHED BY ALFRED A. KNOPF

www.aaknopf.com

Image Credits
© From the personal family photo collection of Lidia Bastianich:
xii, xv, 26, 42, 58, 82, 130, 150, 176
© Tavola Productions: xiii, 179
© Marcus Nilsson: 2

Library of Congress Cataloging-in-Publication Data
Names: Bastianich, Lidia, author. | Manuali, Tanya Bastianich, author. |
Rafael, Armando, photographer.
Title: Lidia's from our family's table to yours : more than 100 recipes
made with love for all occasions / Lidia Matticchio Bastianich and Tanya
Bastianich Manuali ; photographs by Armando Rafael.
Description: New York : Alfred A. Knopf [2023] | Includes index.
Identifiers: LCCN 2022043358 | ISBN 9780525657422 (hardcover) |
ISBN 9780525657439 (ebook)
Subjects: LCSH: Cooking, Italian. | Quick and easy cooking. | LCGFT: Cookbooks.
Classification: LCC TX723 .B31563 2023 | DDC 641.5945—dc23/eng/20220920
LC record available at https://lccn.loc.gov/2022043358

Cover photograph by Armando Rafael
Cover design by Kelly Blair

Manufactured in China
First Edition

From our family to yours.

My life and my profession are tied to my family, and the heartbeat of my family is the kitchen. Food is a connector, an expression of love, of caring, of nourishing, to share not only with family but also with friends and neighbors; it brings people together. In sharing these recipes, these intimate moments and feelings, with you and your dear ones, I also hope to bring to you some of our family's favorite flavors and customs. May your table abound with good food, surrounded by the people you love and who love you in return. So this book is dedicated to you, dear reader; from my family to your friends and family, may many good meals and memories be created.

———————————————

Contents

xi   Introduction

APPETIZERS

6   Panzerotti

7   *Marinara*

8   Mussel Bruschetta

9   Artichokes Braised with Parsley and Prosciutto Cotto

11   Leek and Ricotta Tart

14   Focaccia di Recco

16   Prosciutto and Onion Frittata

17   Kale and Mushroom Frittata

18   Spicy Crispy Roasted Cauliflower

20   Belgian Endive Gratin

21   Vegetable Polpette

23   Eggplant Rollatini

SALADS

29   Celery Salad with Gorgonzola and Chickpeas

31   Grilled Corn, Zucchini, and Tomato Salad

32   Avocado and Tomato Salad with Balsamic and Mozzarella

33   Green Bean, Tuna, and Potato Salad

34   Shredded Beet and Carrot Salad with Apple

35   Warm Escarole Salad with Cannellini Beans and Mackerel

36   Kale Salad with Avocado and Pistachios

39   Chopped Frisée Salad with Salami and Boiled Eggs

40   Red Cabbage Salad with Cubed Crispy Ham

SOUPS

45   Cream of Fava Soup with Rice

46   Pasta and Pea Soup

49   Corn and Bean Soup with Kielbasa

50   Mixed Meat Broth

51   *Shredded Meat Salad*

52   Farro and Bean Soup with Mushrooms

53   Zucchini Soup with Eggs and Cheese

55   Tomato Soup with Fregola and Clams

56   Farina Gnocchi

57   Ricotta Soup

VEGETABLES AND SIDES

62   Asparagus with Lemon Sauce

63   Fennel with Anchovies and Olives

65   Stewed Eggplant and Peppers

66   Rosemary Chickpeas

67 Crispy Baked Zucchini, Carrots, and Cherry Tomatoes

68 Butternut Squash and Cannellini Beans

70 Corn and Greens with Prosciutto Cotto

71 Onion and Potato Gratin

73 Smashed Garlic Rosemary Potatoes

74 Roasted Celery, Carrots, and Onions

75 Braised Cabbage with Onion and Garlic

76 Roasted Spaghetti Squash with Spicy Tomato Sauce

78 Cider-Roasted Apples

79 Roasted Onion Salad

81 Fava Beans with Mint

PASTA, POLENTA, CRESPELLE, AND RISOTTO

86 Crespelle

87 Crespelle with Herb Pesto

89 Crespelle Manicotti with Spinach

90 Mushroom Ragù with Greens over Polenta

92 Risotto with Asparagus and Favas

93 Pumpkin Risotto

94 Shrimp and Tomato Risotto

96 Barley Risotto with Cabbage and Sausage

97 Fresh Pasta for Pappardelle/Tagliatelle/Quadrucci/Fuzi/Pasutice/Anolini

100 Fuzi with Chicken Ragù

103 Istrian Pasutice with Mixed Seafood

104 Pappardelle with Lamb Ragù

106 Ricotta Cavatelli with Arugula

108 Gnocchi with Sauce from Erice

110 Sweet Potato Chickpea Gnocchi with Gorgonzola

112 Timballo with Sausage Ragù

115 Spaghetti in Lemon Cream Sauce

116 Bucatini with Broccoli Walnut Pesto

117 Spicy Lobster Linguine

120 Spaghetti with Mixed Spring Vegetables

121 Fettuccine with Caramelized Onions, Bacon, and Olives

122 Penne Rigate with Sausage, Mushrooms, and Ricotta

123 Rigatoni with Turkey Meatballs

125 Rigatoni with Sausage and Cabbage

126 Spaghetti with Roasted Cherry Tomato Sauce

128 Four-Cheese Baked Macaroni

129 Breakfast Pasta Frittata

FISH AND SHELLFISH

133 Stuffed Calamari in Tomato Sauce

135 Turbot Woodsman-Style

136 Fillet of Sole in Lemon Sauce

139 Seafood Salad

140 Halibut Baked in Parchment Paper

141 Marinated Monkfish Medallions

142 Cuttlefish Salad with Potatoes and Olives

145 Manila Clams Triestina

146 Mussels in Red Sauce with Linguine

147 Grouper in Crazy Water

148 Baked Fresh Sardines

MEAT AND POULTRY

153   Rabbit in Tomato Sauce with Peppers

154   Pork Chops with Mushrooms
      and Pickled Peperoncini

156   Sausages with Mixed Greens

157   Spicy Vinegar Ribs and Potatoes

159   Roast Boneless Leg of Lamb

160   Lamb Stew with Peas

161   Liver Venetian-Style

162   Goulash

164   Beef Rollatini

167   Cheesy Baked Chicken Wings

168   Chicken Scaloppine with Prosciutto and Peas

169   Lidia's Simple Roast Chicken

172   Chicken Rollatini with Fontina and Artichokes

173   Turkey Stuffed Peppers

174   Roast Pork Shoulder

DESSERTS

180   St. Joseph's Zeppole

183   Strawberry and Cream Parfaits

184   "Cat Tongue" Cookies

185   Apricot Jam Half-Moons

186   Rum Raisin Semifreddo

188   Kaiserschmarrn

190   Chocolate Ricotta Brick Cake

191   Chocolate Cherry Panettone

195   Chocolate Amaretti

196   Roasted Cranberries and Pears
      over Ice Cream

197   Mimosa Cake

201   Acknowledgments

203   Index

Introduction

There is no doubt that sharing food brings out the best in people. This book shares some of the wonderful memories, flavors, and festivities that food has brought to my family. My hope is that these recipes and stories will help you create your own special family connections, joyous moments that will last a lifetime and beyond.

The foods that are part of our celebrations become an integral part of our times together. The dishes we share with others become dear to us, just like those they share with us. That is because sharing equates to love. In my house, Panzerotti (page 6) stuffed with mozzarella and ham, shaped like a half-moon, and fried, and Focaccia di Recco (page 14) filled with oozing cheese—almost like a pizza—have always been favorites, first with my children, Joseph and Tanya, and now with my grandchildren, Olivia, Lorenzo, Miles, Ethan, and Julia. I can't make them fast enough—they disappear instantly—or often enough. If it is a holiday meal, there is always a pot of Mixed Meat Broth (page 50) served with tortellini or rice and plenty of grated cheese. A pasta or risotto as an in-between course works for people of any age. Baked pastas like Crespelle Manicotti with Spinach (page 89) or Timballo with Sausage Ragù (page 112) are easy to make for large crowds and are wildly popular. For a main course, the oven is usually on for Lidia's Simple Roast Chicken (page 169) or Roast Pork Shoulder with onions and celery (page 174). There are always some potatoes on the side, like the Smashed Garlic Rosemary Potatoes (page 73), and plenty of vegetables—like Roasted Onion Salad (page 79) or Fava Beans with Mint (page 81). Old favorites are always appreciated, but new tastes create new memories that can also last forever. Desserts, of course, are essential. While the oven is on, in go the Roasted Cranberries and Pears (page 196), to be spooned over ice cream and adored by all.

When I was young, my family lived in a refugee camp in Trieste for two years, having escaped the Yugoslavian communist occupation of Istria. There, Aunt Nina and Uncle Rapetti, who was a fisherman at heart, would make a dish for us I call Manila Clams Triestina (page 145), but using the *vongole veraci* (short-necked clam) of Trieste. In my later travels, I have also discovered and come to love Rabbit in Tomato Sauce with Peppers (page 153) and Liver Venetian-Style (page 161). I know that some people might not be drawn to those, but don't resist them; try to embrace them. Nonna Rosa always prepared dishes with a mound of polenta on the side to help mop up the sauce. Of course, the meals would be accompanied by seasonal vegetables. Sometimes the vegetables would even be the main course. Artichokes Braised with Parsley and Prosciutto Cotto (page 9) and Stewed Eggplant and Peppers (page 65) have always been greeted with cheers around my family table. Fortunately, my kids and grandkids appreciate salads. These, too, are seasonal, and can be served sometimes as a *contorno,* or side dish, sometimes as a whole meal. I never seem to make enough Celery Salad with Gorgonzola and Chickpeas (page 29) or Warm Escarole Salad with Cannellini Beans and Mackerel (page 35). They are gobbled up as soon as they get to the table.

This book is a collection of the recipes that most often grace my table

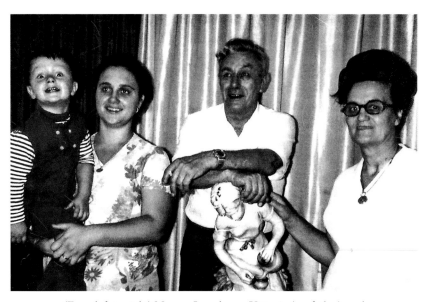

(From left to right) My son, Joseph; me; Vittorio (my father); and
Erminia (my mother), in my mother's apartment in Astoria, 1969

when family are visiting. They are the dishes that I cook for them to express my love, and I share them with you here in the hope that they will become favorites of yours as well. In addition to recipes that we all enjoy, I've included the personal favorites of different family members. When my mother, Grandma Erminia, was with us, especially as she got older, I always tried to please her taste buds. She ate—and appreciated—everything, but particularly loved her Eggplant Rollatini (page 23), Ricotta Soup (page 57), and Chocolate Ricotta Brick Cake (page 190), and I think of her every time I make them. In fact, anything that had ricotta was a go-to food for her. She also loved to help me in the kitchen. I can't tell you how many times we made Fuzi with Chicken Ragù (page 100), one of the Sunday dishes her own mother, Nonna Rosa, made for her family. She cherished the flavors and aromas of her childhood, and we would begin in the morning by making the fuzi, a penne-like fresh pasta, on the kitchen table as she did with her mother. My mother would often take my children when they were small—and, later, my grandchildren—into the kitchen to make gnocchi and Apricot Jam Half-Moons (page 185) together. Eating

Grandkids in my kitchen, 2005: (from left to right)
Miles, Julia, me, Ethan, Lorenzo, and Olivia

together is not the only way for families to bond. Cooking together also creates a special connection. My children and grandchildren will never forget the times they spent in the kitchen with Grandma; certain aromas will forever trigger their memories. Often just a whiff will transport us back to a special place, a special time.

The message sent through each favorite dish is "I love you." Food at our house also carries memories of days with Grandma Erminia and her best-loved foods. She knew all of our own favorites and cooked them for us with love. Now, when I return from a trip, Grandma is no longer there waiting for me. As I open the door, I miss the aroma of the soup she always had for me on the stove. Because Grandma loved eggplant and ricotta, on her special days I would make eggplant rollatini with lots of melting cheese (she *loved* cheese), and manicotti filled with ricotta as well. I always made the Mimosa Cake (page 197) in my mother's honor; it's known in Italy as the cake to celebrate Women's Day, March 8, so the honor was shared by all the women and mothers in our household. My mother loved all desserts, but that cake in particular reminded her of Italy. In Italy, the mimosa flower, a cluster of small bright-yellow puffs, represents the feminine world. Though it looks very delicate, it is actually quite resilient and able to grow in tough terrain. This book is, in part, a celebration of all the joy my mother brought me and the rest of the family through her food.

In this book you will find not only the recipes I cook and eat every day but also those I make when celebrating special holidays. For Christmas at our house, one dish that is never missing is a simmering pot of capon or chicken soup, and we love to have the Farina Gnocchi (page 56) floating in it, a taste that brings me to my grandmother's house in Istria. At Easter it is always roast-lamb time, with lots of rosemary in the lamb and in the potatoes, such as Roast Boneless Leg of Lamb (page 159) and Smashed Garlic Rosemary Potatoes (page 73), and of course Easter dinner also includes the favas that are in season, Fava Beans with Mint (page 81). Thanksgiving is a special holiday for us—an American holiday that we love, our way of thanking and celebrating America. But of course we always add an Italian touch to the meal, usually with a pasta course, like Crespelle Manicotti with Spinach (page 89), which everyone enjoys.

Joseph and Tanya have their favorites, of course. They love antipasto in the form of a Chopped Frisée Salad with Salami and Boiled Eggs (page 39). Their pasta of choice is Spicy Lobster Linguine (page 117). They also

My son, Joseph; me; and my daughter, Tanya,
in front of our home in Astoria, Queens, 1974

like their Stuffed Calamari (page 133), and everyone loves Spicy Vinegar Ribs and Potatoes (page 157). The grandchildren, now young adults, also have favorites of their own. They love their Panzerotti (page 6) and their salads, like Avocado and Tomato Salad with Balsamic and Mozzarella (page 32). They do oscillate between being vegetarians, pescatarians, and back to eaters of everything put in front of them. I am very happy to see that they are extremely conscious of the nutritional value of food, and are concerned about the environmental effects of what we eat. They are all compassionate and well aware of the lack of food for some people on this planet. The pleasures of sharing and giving can of course extend far beyond just the family.

Then there are the recipes that I cook as a special gift on birthdays and special occasions for each one of my grandchildren. Besides Panzerotti, Julia also likes Spaghetti with Roasted Cherry Tomato Sauce (page 126), and Olivia loves Kale Salad with Avocado and Pistachios (page 36) and Manila Clams Triestina (page 145). Miles loves his meat, Spicy Vinegar Ribs and Potatoes (page 157) with some Four-Cheese Baked Macaroni (page 128). Ethan is happy with a nice plate of Spicy Lobster Linguine (page 117), and Roasted Cranberries and Pears over Ice Cream (page 196) as a finale. Lorenzo, on the other hand, likes to begin his meal with Cuttlefish Salad with Potatoes and Olives (page 142). He loves octopus dressed the same way, followed by some crispy Cheesy Baked Chicken Wings (page 167), and then his favorite on the slopes, the skiing dessert, Kaiserschmarrn (page 188).

There are plenty of old favorites in these pages, but I am open to change and hope to keep discovering new, unexpected pleasures. As I travel through Italy, I constantly discover new regional pastas. There are infinite ways to prepare pasta on the Italian Peninsula. One of the recipes I love most is Ricotta Cavatelli with Arugula (page 106). I had it for the first time in Puglia, at the heel of Italy, and I have been making it ever since. I often crave octopus salad, and the sweet meatiness of Cuttlefish Salad with Potatoes and Olives (page 142) is one of my specialties. And what could be better than dunking crispy semolina bread into the sauce of the Manila Clams Triestina (page 145)? These dishes have all become part of my home repertoire and are loved by family members young and old.

I could go on and on listing more and more favorite recipes. This cookbook has many special-occasion foods that are important to my family, but it is also filled with recipes I cook every day, traditional and contemporary variations that grace our table. I think of this book as a love letter to my family. I hope it will get them to remember the smells, the flavors, and the good times we have had eating and cooking together.

But I also think of this book as a love letter to you and to your family. Not long ago, I received an email from a woman from Arizona. She wrote to tell me that, the previous night, four children, Grandma, and Grandpa had all enjoyed a meal of my recipes. She even served the food my way, family-style: *tutti a tavola a mangiare* they went. A day later, and so many miles away, reading that email, I felt I was with them. What an honor to be able to join families across the country through my recipes, and share the sentiments of love and togetherness that food brings. Thank you for inviting me into your home.

— LIDIA'S FROM OUR —

FAMILY TABLE

— TO YOURS —

Grandma Erminia and me playing cards and
having an espresso at my house, 2018

APPETIZERS

In our house, antipasto—appetizers—are almost always served buffet-style. There are lots of vegetables, such as Vegetable Polpette (page 21) and Eggplant Rollatini (page 23), as well as fish dishes—I particularly love having the Marinated Monkfish Medallions (page 141) or another fish "saor" preparation. I often serve canned fish, like anchovies over roasted peppers.

My mother, Grandma Erminia, loved antipasto, but she wasn't a fan of the canned fish. Sitting in her usual seat to my left, she liked to be served. I knew exactly what she wanted, but I would ask her anyway, and her reply was always the same: "I would like to taste a little bit of everything . . . not too much, because I need room for the rest of the meal." And I would make a plate of all her favorites—with a little extra mortadella.

In addition to all the prepared dishes, I also like to have cold cuts like prosciutto, mortadella, capocollo, prosciutto cotto, and salami on the buffet, as well as a selection of cheeses: mozzarella, burrata, Gorgonzola, provola, and a big chunk of Grana Padano.

Panzerotti   6

Marinara   7

Mussel Bruschetta   8

Artichokes Braised with Parsley and Prosciutto Cotto   9

Leek and Ricotta Tart   11

Focaccia di Recco   14

Prosciutto and Onion Frittata   16

Kale and Mushroom Frittata   17

Spicy Crispy Roasted Cauliflower   18

Belgian Endive Gratin   20

Vegetable Polpette   21

Eggplant Rollatini   23

Panzerotti

Makes about 1 dozen

FOR THE DOUGH

2 cups all-purpose flour, plus more for working the dough

1½ teaspoons instant yeast

1½ teaspoons kosher salt

2 tablespoons extra-virgin olive oil, plus more for the bowl

FOR THE FILLING

8 ounces mild provola or low-moisture mozzarella, shredded

4 ounces prosciutto cotto, thickly sliced, cut into matchsticks

½ cup freshly grated Grana Padano

¼ cup chopped fresh basil leaves

Vegetable oil, for frying

Marinara (recipe follows), warmed, for serving

My son-in-law, Corrado Manuali, is Roman. His father's second wife, Anna, took great care of Corrado and his sister Francesca. Anna is Sicilian and loves to cook, and that tradition has continued to the next generation, Lorenzo and Julia. Panzerotti is their favorite thing that Anna makes. It's easy, delicious, and a crowd pleaser.

For the dough: Combine the flour, yeast, and salt in the bowl of a mixer fitted with the paddle attachment. Combine the olive oil and ¾ cup cold water in a spouted measuring cup. Pour combined liquids into the flour. Mix on low speed. Knead on medium-high speed until the dough forms a ball and is smooth and springy, 5 to 6 minutes.

Scrape the dough onto a floured surface, and knead until the dough comes together in a smooth ball. Coat a large bowl with olive oil, then add the dough. Cover, and let rise at room temperature until doubled in size, about 1½ hours.

While the dough rises, make the filling: Combine the provola, prosciutto cotto, Grana Padano, and basil in a medium bowl, using your hands to toss and squeeze until the mixture comes together in a loose mass.

Once the dough has risen, punch it down. On a floured work surface, roll the dough to about ¼ inch thick. Use a 4½-inch round cutter to cut the dough into as many rounds as you can fit in. Divide the filling among the rounds, and wet the edges of each circle with your finger dipped in water or with a pastry brush. Press with your fingers to seal the edges in a half-moon shape. Place on a parchment-lined baking sheet, roll out the dough scraps once more, and cut out more circles. (You'll have about twelve in all.) Let them sit while the oil for frying heats, 10 to 15 minutes.

Heat 3 inches of vegetable oil in a large Dutch oven to 350 degrees Fahrenheit. Add half of the panzerotti and fry, turning occasionally, until they're puffed and golden, about 5 minutes. Drain on a paper-towel-lined tray, and repeat with the second batch. Serve warm, with marinara.

Marinara

Makes about 3 cups

3 tablespoons extra-virgin olive oil

5 garlic cloves, thinly sliced

One 28-ounce can whole
San Marzano tomatoes,
crushed by hand

1 teaspoon kosher salt,
plus more to taste

¼ teaspoon peperoncino flakes

2 leafy sprigs fresh basil

This is my go-to quick-and-easy marinara sauce, and I use it in countless ways. I always have a few pints of it in my freezer; it's an easy anchor to start so many meals—a pasta dish, a skillet gratinate, or a baked, layered lasagna or parmigiana. You can double or triple this recipe and stock your freezer, too. A frozen quart of marinara with a bow tied to it makes a much-appreciated gift when you're visiting older parents, sick friends, or kids away at school. Do not forget a pound or two of pasta to complete the gift. They'll remember you long after you have said goodbye.

Heat the oil in a large skillet over medium heat. Add the garlic, and stir just until it begins to sizzle (don't let it brown), about 30 seconds. Add the tomatoes and 1 cup water from the tomato can. Add the salt and peperoncino, and tuck in the basil sprigs. Bring the mixture to a simmer, and cook until it's thickened and flavorful, about 15 minutes. Season with more salt, if needed. Remove and discard the basil sprigs.

Mussel Bruschetta

Bruschetta con Cozze

Serves 4

8 thick slices country bread
(about 3 inches long)

1 garlic clove, crushed and peeled

¼ cup extra-virgin olive oil,
plus more for brushing

Kosher salt

1 small onion, chopped

1 small red bell pepper,
seeded, chopped

6 scallions, chopped, white
and green parts separated

¼ teaspoon peperoncino flakes

1 cup dry white wine

2 pounds mussels, scrubbed

Gianfranco, Tanya's father-in-law, is from Rome, and has a summer home on the beach in Fiumicino, just outside the Leonardo da Vinci Airport. Whenever I fly into or out of Rome and I have some time, I go and visit with him. The sandy coastline is where the Romans cool off in the summer, and it is lined with chairs and beach umbrellas from the different beach clubs and beachfront restaurants. We usually end up having lunch at a place that has been there forever. The food is simple, straightforward, and all about the fresh fish of the area. They offer great appetizers, and one of my favorites is the clam bruschetta or mussel bruschetta. This is my version, and it always makes me think fondly of my long lunches with Gianfranco.

Heat a grill pan over medium-low heat. Add the bread (in batches if necessary), and grill until golden and crisp, 3 to 4 minutes per side. While they're still hot, rub both sides with the crushed garlic clove, and brush one side lightly with olive oil. Season that same side lightly with salt. Set aside.

Heat the ¼ cup olive oil in a large Dutch oven over medium heat. Add the onion, bell pepper, and scallion whites, and cook until they're softened, about 5 minutes. Add the peperoncino, and cook until everything is sizzling, about 1 minute. Add the white wine, and bring it to a boil. Add the mussels, toss, and bring the liquid to a simmer. Cover, and cook until the mussels open, about 5 minutes. Discard any that do not open. Turn off the heat, and let them cool just until you can touch the shells; then pluck the mussels from their shells and return the mussels to the sauce in the Dutch oven. Return the liquid to a simmer, and cook to reduce the juices until they're syrupy, about 3 minutes. Season with salt if needed, and stir in the scallion greens.

Lay the grilled bread on a serving platter, and top with the mussels and their juices.

Artichokes Braised with Parsley and Prosciutto Cotto

Carciofi con Prezzemolo e Prosciutto Cotto

Serves 4 to 6

2 lemons, 1 halved, peeled in long strips with a vegetable peeler, then juiced

2½ pounds small (not baby) artichokes (about 12)

¼ cup extra-virgin olive oil, plus more for drizzling

8 ounces prosciutto cotto, thickly sliced, diced

1 medium onion, chopped

3 garlic cloves, sliced

3 sprigs fresh thyme

2 fresh bay leaves

Pinch of peperoncino flakes

Kosher salt

1 cup dry white wine

2 cups low-sodium chicken stock, or as needed

¼ cup chopped fresh Italian parsley

My Roman son-in-law, Corrado, absolutely loves artichokes, and I do, too. We enjoy eating them together, nibbling on every leaf and licking the juices off our fingers. It takes some effort, but the sweetness of the artichoke is totally worth it. During artichoke season around Rome, February to April, you will see huge piles of enormous artichokes along the side of the country roads, where local farmers are selling their bounty. Artichokes are one of Italy's most beloved vegetables. It takes a bit more work to clean them than some others, but once you have gotten the knack of it, you will cook them often. Although we can buy artichokes year-round, in Italy they are best in early spring. The leaves are tender and the choke is almost nonexistent. This preparation is an offshoot of a traditional Roman recipe, and if you travel to Rome in May you are bound to find it in every trattoria and restaurant. I add some prosciutto cotto to turn it into a great appetizer, or even a main course if you throw in some fregola at the end of the cooking process.

Fill a large bowl with cold water, squeeze in the juice from the halved lemon, and add the halves to the water. Working with 1 artichoke at a time, snap off the tough outer leaves until you reach the pale, tender leaves inside. Trim the tip of the stem, and peel off the stem's tough exterior. Use a serrated knife to cut off the top third of the artichoke. Cut the remainder in half vertically, and scrape out the choke with a spoon. Add artichokes to the lemon water.

Heat the olive oil over medium heat in a medium Dutch oven. Add the prosciutto cotto, and cook until the edges begin to crisp, about 2 minutes. Add the onion, and cook, stirring occasionally, until it's wilted, about 4 minutes.

Drain the artichokes and pat them dry. Add them to the pan, along with the garlic, thyme, bay leaves, peperoncino, lemon peel, and 1 teaspoon salt. Toss to coat the artichokes in the oil. Add the wine and juice and peel of the second lemon and bring to a simmer. Simmer rapidly to reduce by →

← half, about 2 minutes. Add enough chicken stock to come about halfway up the sides of the artichokes. Adjust the heat so the liquid is simmering, cover, and cook, stirring once or twice, until the artichokes are tender all the way through, about 20 minutes. Uncover, bring the liquid to a boil, and simmer to reduce the juices by about half, 2 to 3 minutes. Discard the bay leaves, stir in the parsley, drizzle with more olive oil, and serve.

Leek and Ricotta Tart

Crostata di Porri e Ricotta

Serves 6 to 8

FOR THE DOUGH

1½ cups all-purpose flour, plus more as needed

¼ cup freshly grated Grana Padano

2 teaspoons sugar

½ teaspoon kosher salt

1 large egg yolk (save the white for the filling)

7 tablespoons unsalted butter, cold, cut into bits

FOR THE FILLING

3 tablespoons unsalted butter, plus more for the baking pan

2 large leeks, white and light-green parts, halved vertically, sliced ½ inch thick

4 scallions, chopped

Kosher salt and freshly ground black pepper

1 large egg white (yolk used in dough)

1 cup good-quality fresh ricotta

½ cup freshly grated Grana Padano, plus more for sprinkling

¼ cup chopped fresh Italian parsley

Pinch of freshly grated nutmeg

1 large egg, beaten, for an egg wash

When I was growing up, in the springtime, when my grandma's goats were kidding, there was always abundant goat milk, and Nonna Rosa, my mother's mother, made loads of ricotta on those spring days. We ate ricotta for breakfast, for dessert, and as a snack, and we made stuffed pastas, ricotta gnocchi, cheesecakes, and tarts with it. On Sundays, when my grandma had a little more time, she would bake, and a ricotta tart like this one was easy and fast. She made it with different spring vegetables from the garden, but one of my favorites was this version, with leeks. The kid goats were my pets, and I loved playing with them. Nonna Rosa had a pile of old clothes, which she ripped into strips and used to tie the tomato plants, the artichokes, and other vegetables. But we used the cloth strips to tie decorative bows on the kids and on the foals, when we were lucky enough to catch one.

For the dough: Combine the flour, grated cheese, sugar, and salt in a food processor, and pulse to combine. Beat the egg yolk in a spouted measuring cup with ⅓ cup cold water.

Scatter the butter pieces over the flour, and pulse until the mixture is lumpy. Drizzle in the egg-yolk mixture, and pulse just until the dough comes together, adding a little more water or flour if needed. Move the dough to a floured counter, and knead it a few times to bring it together. Form it into a disk, wrap in plastic wrap, and chill until just firm, about 1 hour.

For the filling: Melt the 3 tablespoons butter in a medium skillet over medium heat. Add the leeks, and cook, stirring often, until they're tender, about 10 minutes. Add the scallions, and continue to cook until they are wilted but the green parts are still bright green, about 4 minutes. Season with ½ teaspoon salt and several grinds of pepper, and let it cool.

Beat the egg white in a large bowl until foamy. Add the cooled leeks, the ricotta, ½ cup grated cheese, parsley, and nutmeg. Season with ½ teaspoon salt. Stir to combine. →

← Preheat the oven to 375 degrees with a rack in the bottom third. Butter a 9-inch cake pan. Roll the dough on a piece of parchment to a circle about 12 to 13 inches in diameter, and lay it in the buttered pan. Add the filling, and spread it to an even layer. Fold the overhanging edges in to make a crust on the edges. Brush the crust with the egg wash, and sprinkle all over with grated Grana Padano.

Bake until the filling is set and deep golden brown and the crust is golden on the edges, 40 to 50 minutes. Remove to a rack to cool. Serve it warm or at room temperature, cut into wedges.

Focaccia di Recco

Makes 2

1¼ pounds stracchino
or crescenza cheese

2 cups bread flour,
plus more as needed

1 teaspoon kosher salt,
plus more for sprinkling

⅓ cup extra-virgin olive oil, plus
more for the pans and as needed

Everyone loves the smell of baking focaccia. I enjoy making it when my family comes over or I have other guests. I often put out a large antipasto spread as an appetizer, and my freshly baked focaccia adds an extra-special homemade touch to the spread. I often bake it plain, but sometimes I top it with tomatoes, or olives, or onions . . . or all three! Focaccia is popular all over Italy. It can have different toppings, seasonings, and textures depending on the region, but one of my favorites, different and super-delicious, is the focaccia di Recco. Recco is a city on the Ligurian coast, near Genova, known for its focaccia as well as for pansotti (a special kind of pasta dressed with walnut sauce) and the famous trofiette pasta with pesto. If you happen to be in the area in September, you can watch a spectacular fireworks display and enjoy the specialties and delicious street food along the beautiful Riviera. This focaccia is a bit different: it is not topped, but, rather, filled with stracchino, a cow's milk cheese from the north of Italy, which is not aged, eaten young, and usually has no rind. It is a soft cheese with a mild, delicate flavor. If you cannot find stracchino or crescenza, you could substitute an equal amount of a young, ripe Brie, with the rind removed.

Break up the cheese by pulling it apart a bit, in a strainer lined with cheesecloth over a bowl. Let it drain in the refrigerator for a couple of hours.

Combine the flour and salt in the food processor, and pulse to combine. Combine ½ cup plus 2 tablespoons cold water and ⅓ cup olive oil in a spouted measuring cup. With the processor running, add the water mixture, and process until the mixture forms a loose ball on the blade. Continue to process until the dough is smooth and elastic, about 1 minute. Put the dough on a floured counter, knead it a few times to bring it together, and wrap it in plastic wrap. Let it rest at room temperature for 1 hour.

Preheat your oven to 500 degrees (or as high as it will go).

Brush two 11-to-12-inch pizza pans liberally with a tablespoon of olive oil each. Divide the dough into quarters. Roll or stretch one piece of dough into an 11-to-12-inch round. (Roll it as thin as possible without its tearing, as thin as pasta dough if you can.) Set that piece of dough in one pizza pan, and drop half of the cheese in small lumps over the top, leaving a scant 1-inch border. Brush the edge of the border with water. Roll out a second piece of dough in the same way, and lay it over the top of the first. Press the edges to seal. (For a neater look, you can run a pizza cutter around the border to make a perfect round.) Cut a few small slits in the top of the dough to help steam escape. Brush with olive oil and sprinkle with salt. Repeat with the remaining ingredients in the second pan.

Bake on the bottom rack until the bottom and top of each focaccia is crisp and golden, 16 to 18 minutes. Brush once more, liberally, with olive oil, and serve warm.

Prosciutto and Onion Frittata

Frittata di Prosciutto e Cipolla

Serves 2 or 3

3 tablespoons extra-virgin olive oil

4 ounces prosciutto crudo
or prosciutto ends, thickly
sliced, cut into matchsticks

1 medium spring onion, white
and green parts thinly sliced,
or 4 scallions, chopped

6 large eggs

Kosher salt

Country bread, for serving

Freshly ground black pepper

My maternal grandfather, Giovanni, loved frittatas, and this one was his favorite. We had chickens growing up, so eggs were always available, and onions were always growing in the garden or hanging, braided, in the *cantina* (cellar). My grandpa and grandma raised two pigs every year, so we had prosciutto. When Grandpa cut some prosciutto, he would always save the fattier corner pieces to make this frittata. What's unique about this frittata is the cooking time. He liked it soft and runny, and I still make it that way. If any was left over, it made its way between two slices of bread for *merenda* (snack) or lunch the next day.

Heat the olive oil in a large nonstick skillet over medium-low heat. Add the prosciutto, and cook until the fat begins to render, about 2 minutes. Add the spring onions or scallions, and cook until they're wilted, about 3 minutes.

Beat the eggs in a medium bowl with ½ teaspoon salt. Pour the eggs into the skillet, and use a wooden spoon to evenly distribute them over the ingredients in the pan. Cook until loosely set, about 2 minutes. Remove from the heat. (The eggs will finish cooking in the pan.)

Mound the frittata on bread, grind some pepper over the top, and serve.

Kale and Mushroom Frittata

Frittata di Cavolo Nero e Funghi

Serves 4

6 tablespoons extra-virgin olive oil

1 small onion, chopped

10 ounces cremini mushrooms, thickly sliced

1 small bunch kale or other hearty greens (dandelion, Swiss chard, arugula, spinach, etc.), about 6 cups

Kosher salt

8 large eggs

¼ teaspoon peperoncino flakes

When I was growing up, in the springtime, before the garden began to produce, nature was our source of wild greens. Nonna Rosa made soups, pastas, and delicious frittatas with what we foraged: the young shoots of nettles and wild asparagus, fennel fronds, ramps, and chives in the fields, as well as spring mushrooms like champignons, morels, and chanterelles. But if you are more city-bound, you can add any greens or mushrooms you like to this frittata, and since kale is in vogue, I thought, why not make a kale frittata? In this case, the mushrooms sweeten the kale a bit, making the dish both nutritious and delicious.

Preheat the oven to 375 degrees.

Heat a medium (10-inch) nonstick skillet over medium heat. Add ¼ cup of the olive oil. Add the onion, and cook until it begins to soften, 3 to 4 minutes. Add the mushrooms, and cook, stirring occasionally, until they release their liquid, about 5 minutes. Add the kale, and season with ½ teaspoon salt. Pour in ½ cup water. Cover, and cook until the greens are tender, about 8 minutes. Uncover, increase the heat, and cook to reduce any excess liquid away.

Remove the vegetables to a bowl, and wipe the skillet clean. Return it to medium heat, and add the remaining olive oil. Beat the eggs in a large bowl with 1 teaspoon salt and the peperoncino.

When the oil is hot, pour in the egg mixture, and let it cook for a minute or two; then spread the greens evenly over the top. Cook on the stovetop just until the sides begin to set, about 5 minutes. Transfer to the oven (or, if you're feeling brave, invert it and return it to the skillet to finish on the stovetop), and bake until cooked through, 10 to 12 minutes.

Slide the frittata onto a cutting board, and cut into wedges. Serve it warm or at room temperature.

Spicy Crispy Roasted Cauliflower

Cavolfiore Croccante al Forno

Serves 4 to 6

¾ cup fine dried bread crumbs

¾ cup freshly grated pecorino or Grana Padano, or a combination

1 teaspoon garlic powder

1 teaspoon onion powder

Kosher salt

1 stick unsalted butter, melted

1 medium head cauliflower, cut into florets

Marinara (page 7), warmed, for dipping

I love cauliflower in pasta sauces, salads, and soups, and braised in tomato sauce. But I know that not everyone feels the same way. I've found that making it crispy in the oven, as in this recipe, opens the door for many cauliflower doubters. These bite-sized florets can be finger food for gatherings, served as an appetizer, or as an added vegetable for the table. It was a dish I made for my grandkids when they were younger, a good alternative to a lot of the less healthy fried finger foods often served to young children. They gobbled them up, loving every bite of the crispy florets, which you can serve sprinkled with some lemon juice or dunked in one of your family's favorite sauces. But if all else fails, ketchup with some Calabrese peperoncino is spicy goodness.

Preheat the oven to 425 degrees. Line two baking sheets with parchment.

Combine the bread crumbs, cheese, garlic and onion powders, and ½ teaspoon salt in a large bowl.

Pour the melted butter into a second large bowl. Add the cauliflower, season it with ½ teaspoon salt, and toss to coat in the butter.

Add half of the cauliflower to the crumbs, and toss well to coat thoroughly. Place on one of the baking sheets. Repeat with the remaining cauliflower and crumbs. Sprinkle any remaining crumbs in the bowl on top of the florets.

Bake the cauliflower until it's deep golden brown and crispy, about 30 minutes. Serve it warm with the marinara for dipping.

Belgian Endive Gratin

Indivia Belga Gratinata

Serves 4 to 6

4 tablespoons unsalted butter

2 tablespoons all-purpose flour

2 cups whole milk

Kosher salt

4 large or 6 small heads Belgian endive, halved lengthwise

8 ounces prosciutto cotto, thickly sliced, diced

½ cup dry white wine

1 cup grated Italian Fontina

¼ cup freshly grated Grana Padano

I like sweet and crunchy Belgian endive in salads. It reminds me of the radicchio trevisano that I ate when I was growing up, which has a similar crunchy consistency. It is in the chicory family, and you can find it year-round, but it is especially delicious baked in the winter, and great for family gatherings; just bring the whole bubbling tray to the table. It can be served as an appetizer, as a side dish, or even as a whole meal.

Preheat the oven to 400 degrees.

Melt 2 tablespoons of the butter in a medium saucepan over medium heat. When the butter is melted, sprinkle in the flour, and stir to make a paste. Cook and stir to remove the raw-flour smell, 1 to 2 minutes. Whisk in the milk, and season with ½ teaspoon salt. Bring to a simmer, and cook until it's thickened, 5 to 7 minutes. Set aside and keep it warm.

Melt the remaining 2 tablespoons butter in a large skillet over medium heat. Add the endive, and cook, turning occasionally, until it's browned all over, about 4 minutes. Sprinkle in the ham cubes, and let them brown for a minute or two. Season with ½ teaspoon salt. Pour in the wine, and simmer until it's syrupy, about 2 minutes.

Pour the sauce through a strainer over the endive. Sprinkle with the Fontina and Grana Padano. Bake in the oven until browned and bubbly on top, about 20 minutes.

Vegetable Polpette

Polpette di Verdura

Makes about 18

2 small zucchini (about 10 ounces)

1 medium russet potato, peeled (about 8 ounces)

2 large eggs, beaten

1½ cups panko bread crumbs

1½ cups freshly grated Grana Padano

½ cup chopped fresh Italian parsley

2 scallions, finely chopped

1 teaspoon grated lemon zest

Kosher salt and freshly ground black pepper

Vegetable oil, for frying

Marinara (page 7), warmed, or lemon wedges, for serving

Today we are all trying to eat more vegetables, but Italians in general, and particularly my family, have always been big on them. For us, they are just as important as proteins. Here is one rendition that my brother and I loved as kids; they look like regular meat *polpette* and taste even better. Meat was scarce, but vegetables from our family garden abundant. We made sandwiches with the vegetable balls, and off to the beach we went.

Grate the zucchini and potato on the coarse holes of a box grater, place in a kitchen towel, and wring out any excess moisture. Transfer to a large bowl, and add the eggs, bread crumbs, Grana Padano, parsley, scallions, lemon zest, 1 teaspoon salt, and several grinds of pepper. Mix well to combine. Set the mixture aside for 10 to 15 minutes to let the bread crumbs soak up some of the moisture from the vegetables.

Form into 2-inch patties or cylinders, and place these on a parchment-lined baking sheet.

Heat about an inch of vegetable oil in a large nonstick skillet over medium heat. The oil is ready when a little of the zucchini mixture sizzles on contact. Carefully add the *polpette* to the oil. Don't crowd the skillet—cook in 2 batches. Cook, turning the *polpette* occasionally, until they're golden and the vegetables are tender, about 4 minutes per side. Drain them on a paper-towel-lined baking sheet, and season with salt. Repeat with the remaining zucchini mixture. Serve warm or at room temperature, with marinara for dipping or lemon wedges to squeeze over the top.

Eggplant Rollatini

Rollatini di Melanzane

Serves 4 to 6

FOR THE EGGPLANT ROLLATINI

3 small eggplants
(each about 4 inches wide,
about 1 pound total weight)

Vegetable oil, for frying

All-purpose flour, for dredging

Kosher salt

12 ounces good-quality fresh ricotta

6 ounces fresh mozzarella, shredded

1½ cups freshly grated Grana Padano

¼ cup chopped fresh Italian parsley

1 large egg, beaten

FOR THE TOMATO SAUCE

⅓ cup extra-virgin olive oil

3 garlic cloves, sliced

2 pints ripe grape or cherry
tomatoes, halved crosswise

Kosher salt

¼ cup chopped fresh basil

Eggplant rollatini is more of a southern-Italian dish, but although she was from the north, my mother, Grandma Erminia, loved it. Her mother, Rosa, made plenty of ricotta from the milk the family goats gave. Ricotta is so versatile in the kitchen, and I love cooking with it, from appetizers to desserts. It makes everybody happy, but at our house, especially when a bubbling pan of eggplant rollatini is delivered to the table, there are extra-big smiles. I would make these eggplant rollatini for Grandma Erminia on her birthday, and at other times, too, as she got on in age (God blessed her to live to be a hundred). They were light and soft, so easy for her to eat. She always asked if there were some left for tomorrow and I always made sure to have some extra saved for her.

Preheat the oven to 400 degrees.

For the eggplant rollatini: Trim the stems and ends from the eggplants. Remove strips of peel about 1 inch wide from the eggplants, leaving about half the peel intact. Slice the rounded sides from two opposite sides so that the eggplant sliced will lie flat. Slice the now flattened eggplant a scant ½ inch thick lengthwise (to get about sixteen slices). Chop the ends you cut off, and set them aside.

Heat about ½ inch vegetable oil in a large skillet over medium heat until the edge of an eggplant slice sizzles on contact. Spread some flour on a plate. Season the eggplant slices with salt, and dredge them in the flour. Fry, in batches without crowding, until they're tender and golden, about 3 minutes per side. Drain on a paper-towel-lined baking sheet.

For the filling: In a large bowl, combine the ricotta, shredded mozzarella, ½ cup grated Grana Padano, the parsley, and the egg. Season with 1 teaspoon salt, and stir to combine. Lay the eggplant slices out on your work surface with the top end toward you. Divide the filling among the slices, and roll them up.

For the tomato sauce and to serve: Carefully pour the oil out of the skillet and wipe it clean. Add the olive oil, and heat it over medium →

← heat. Add the reserved chopped eggplant, and cook until it's lightly browned, 2 to 3 minutes. Scatter in the garlic, and cook until it's sizzling, about 1 minute. Add the tomatoes, and season with 1 teaspoon salt. Cook, tossing occasionally, until the tomatoes begin to wilt on the edges, 2 to 3 minutes. Add ½ cup water, cover, and simmer until the tomatoes have broken down and the mixture is saucy, 10 to 15 minutes. Stir in the basil.

Nestle the rolls, seam side down, in the sauce, spooning a little of the sauce over each as you go. Sprinkle with the remaining 1 cup grated Grana Padano. Bake until the rollatini are browned and the sauce is bubbly, 25 to 30 minutes.

Antipasto spread, buffet-style, before a
Christmas meal at my house, 2020

SALADS

As much as all generations love antipasto, sometimes salads take their place at our family dinners. The grandchildren, as they've gotten older, have loved salad, and that was the way they wanted to start a meal. Grandma Erminia also liked her salads, particularly ones with bitter chicories, and would complement the bitterness with either boiled potatoes, cannellini beans, or chickpeas. I think of her every time I make the Warm Escarole Salad with Cannellini Beans and Mackerel (page 35). She liked to dress all her salads only with extra-virgin olive oil and wine vinegar—and an extra splash of vinegar at that.

Celery Salad with Gorgonzola and Chickpeas   29

Grilled Corn, Zucchini, and Tomato Salad   31

Avocado and Tomato Salad with Balsamic and Mozzarella   32

Green Bean, Tuna, and Potato Salad   33

Shredded Beet and Carrot Salad with Apple   34

Warm Escarole Salad with Cannellini Beans and Mackerel   35

Kale Salad with Avocado and Pistachios   36

Chopped Frisée Salad with Salami and Boiled Eggs   39

Red Cabbage Salad with Cubed Crispy Ham   40

Celery Salad with Gorgonzola and Chickpeas

Insalata di Sedano con Gorgonzola e Ceci

Serves 4 to 6

Two 15.5-ounce cans chickpeas, drained and rinsed

6 stalks celery, thinly sliced on the bias, plus ½ cup inner celery leaves

1 Granny Smith apple, halved, cored, julienned

½ medium red onion, thinly sliced

3 tablespoons white wine vinegar

¼ cup extra-virgin olive oil

Kosher salt

½ cup chopped walnuts, toasted

6 ounces Gorgonzola Dolce

When my kids and grandkids were little, they would turn their noses up at the smell, but today Gorgonzola is much loved at our house, and I especially like it paired with celery. The flavors balance each other so well, so why not turn it into a salad with the addition of apples and walnuts? Make sure to add the celery leaves as well. I like to use Gorgonzola Dolce, but if you prefer Piccante, by all means use it. The apples will sweeten the cheese a bit, and the chickpeas mellow it as well. This makes a great appetizer, or a lunch with a few slices of prosciutto added.

Combine the chickpeas, celery, apple, and red onion in a serving bowl. Drizzle with the vinegar and oil, and season with 1 teaspoon salt. Toss well to combine. Add the celery leaves and walnuts, and crumble in the Gorgonzola. Toss gently, taking care not to break up the cheese too much. Serve immediately.

Grilled Corn, Zucchini, and Tomato Salad

Insalata di Mais alla Griglia, Zucchine e Pomodori

Serves 6

4 ears corn, shucked

2 medium zucchini, sliced lengthwise into ½-inch-thick planks

1 large red onion, cut into ½-inch-thick rings

4 plum tomatoes, cored, halved lengthwise

2 large portobello mushrooms, stemmed

6 tablespoons extra-virgin olive oil

Kosher salt and freshly ground black pepper

2 tablespoons red wine vinegar

¼ cup chopped fresh basil

Everybody likes grilled vegetables, especially in the summer. My brother, Franco, is the grill master of the family, so when we go to his house in upstate New York, in Dutchess County, he does the grilling. I always have him grill extra vegetables, which I turn into a big salad. This salad is also a good idea when you have leftover grilled vegetables—even the next day, they'll come back to life with the dressing, and if you have some chicken or meat left over, throw it in and you'll have a complete lunch.

Preheat a grill or double-burner grill pan to medium-high heat.

Spread the vegetables on a sheet pan, drizzle them with ¼ cup olive oil, and toss to coat. Season with 2 teaspoons salt and a generous amount of black pepper.

Place the vegetables on the grill (in batches, if space is an issue). Grill, turning occasionally, until the corn is charred, 8 to 10 minutes. Grill the zucchini and red onion, turning occasionally, until they're charred and wilted, 6 to 8 minutes. Grill the portobellos, turning occasionally, until tender, about 10 minutes. Grill the tomatoes, turning occasionally, until they're charred and have just begun to soften, 4 to 5 minutes. Remove all to the baking sheet as they're done.

Cut the corn from the cobs into a large bowl, and add the grilled onion rings. Drizzle over them the remaining 2 tablespoons olive oil and the red wine vinegar. Toss well. Thickly slice the portobellos, and cut the zucchini on the bias into thick "fingers." Arrange the zucchini, tomatoes, and mushrooms around the edge of a large serving platter. Mound the corn and onions in the middle. Season lightly with salt, if needed. Sprinkle the basil over the top.

Avocado and Tomato Salad with Balsamic and Mozzarella

Insalata di Avocado e Pomodori con Aceto Balsamico e Mozzarella

Serves 4 to 6

1 medium shallot, finely chopped

Kosher salt

3 tablespoons balsamic vinegar

⅓ cup extra-virgin olive oil

2 large ripe tomatoes,
cut into chunks

2 ripe avocados, peeled,
cut into chunks

12 ounces mozzarella
bocconcini, halved

2 romaine hearts, chopped

Avocado is ubiquitous in America, and the two younger generations in my family really enjoy it for breakfast with eggs or in a salad for lunch. Avocado is not a traditional Italian fruit, but these days it is plentifully grown in Sicily, where it has become an important element in the economy, so why not make it part of the menu? Avocado and tomato is a marriage made in heaven. Dress it the simple Italian way, top it with some fresh mozzarella, and you have a delicious appetizer, lunch, or dinner. Add some cold cooked shrimp and and you'll make it into a delicious main course.

Combine the shallots, 1½ teaspoons salt, and the balsamic vinegar in a large serving bowl. Whisk in the olive oil. Add the tomatoes, avocados, mozzarella, and romaine. Toss well, and serve immediately.

Green Bean, Tuna, and Potato Salad

Insalata di Fagiolini, Tonno e Patate

Serves 4 to 6

1 pound medium
Yukon Gold potatoes

Kosher salt

12 ounces green beans, trimmed

2 stalks celery, thinly
sliced on the bias

1 small red onion, sliced

3 tablespoons red wine vinegar

¼ cup extra-virgin olive oil

Two 5-ounce cans tuna
in olive oil, drained

In Istria and along the whole Dalmatian coast, boiled potatoes are commonly found in salads. They are usually tossed in while still warm, which really blends all the elements of the salad together wonderfully. Potatoes were plentiful when I was growing up, and were used in a salad to "stretch" the other ingredients. The potatoes fill the plate and the stomach, rounded off with vegetables. Using potatoes and some cooked beans as the base, and adding some onions and canned tuna, makes for a heartier salad for lunch or dinner.

Put the potatoes in a large pot and add water to cover by 2 inches. Season the water with salt. Bring to a simmer, and cook until the potatoes just begin to become tender, 8 to 10 minutes. Add the green beans, and cook until both are tender, 6 to 8 minutes more. Drain. Run the green beans under cold water to cool them, and pat them dry. Place the green beans in a large serving bowl.

Peel the potatoes, cut them into chunks, and add these to the bowl. Add the celery and red onion. Drizzle with the vinegar and olive oil, and season with 1 teaspoon salt. Toss well. Flake in the tuna, and toss to combine.

Shredded Beet and Carrot Salad with Apple

Insalata di Barbabietole, Carote e Mele

Serves 4 to 6

3 tablespoons cider vinegar

Kosher salt and freshly
ground black pepper

1 large shallot, finely chopped

¼ cup extra-virgin olive oil

2 medium beets, peeled, shredded

2 medium carrots, peeled, shredded

2 Granny Smith apples, halved
and cored, cut into matchsticks

¼ cup chopped fresh Italian parsley

Sometimes ideas for recipes come from the most unexpected places. One morning, heading to the restaurant to work, I stopped to get some freshly squeezed juice. The list of possible juices was endless, and there was also an option to create your own combination. That morning, I had decided I was in the mood for carrot and apple juice when the server asked, "Would you like some fresh beet juice in there as well?" I love beets, so I approved. It was delicious. When I got to the restaurant, I went to the kitchen and thought . . . surely a salad of freshly shredded beets, shredded carrots, and some apples would be delicious as well, and it was. So here it is.

In a large serving bowl, whisk together the cider vinegar, 1½ teaspoons salt, and a generous amount of black pepper. Whisk in the shallot, then the olive oil, to make a dressing.

Add the beets, carrots, apple, and parsley. Toss well. Let sit at room temperature for 10 minutes to blend the flavors before serving.

Warm Escarole Salad with Cannellini Beans and Mackerel

Insalata Tiepida di Scarola con Fagioli Cannellini e Sgombro

**Serves 4, plus extra
beans for another day**

1 pound dried cannellini beans

2 fresh bay leaves

1 sprig fresh rosemary

Peperoncino flakes

5 tablespoons extra-virgin olive oil

Kosher salt

3 tablespoons red wine vinegar

1 small red onion, thinly sliced

3 tablespoons capers in brine,
drained

Two 5-ounce cans mackerel
fillets in oil, drained

2 escarole hearts, coarsely
chopped (about 8 cups)

My grandmother used the differing temperatures and textures of boiled potatoes, beans, and vegetables to bring salads to life. I loved her approach, and try to bring it to all the salads I make, especially if they are a main course. Here, the warm cooked beans mellow the escarole leaves and bring out the flavor of the mackerel.

Put the beans in a pot with water to cover by about 2 inches. Refrigerate and soak overnight.

The next day, drain the beans and return them to the pot with fresh water to cover by 2 inches. Add the bay leaves, rosemary, a pinch of peperoncino, and 2 tablespoons of the olive oil. Bring to a simmer over medium-low heat, and cook, uncovered, until the beans are tender throughout but not falling apart, about 1 hour. Season with salt. Discard the bay leaves and rosemary sprig.

Scoop out about 2 heaping cups of the warm beans, letting the liquid drain back into the pot. (Whatever is left in the pot, liquid and beans, can be saved for another meal.) Put the beans in a serving bowl and drizzle with the vinegar and remaining 3 tablespoons olive oil. Season with 1 teaspoon salt. Add the red onion and capers, and toss well to combine. Crumble in the mackerel, and add the escarole. Toss well. Serve immediately.

Kale Salad with Avocado and Pistachios

Insalata di Cavolo Nero con Avocado e Pistacchi

Serves 4 to 6

2 large eggs, hard-boiled

2 tablespoons red wine vinegar

1 tablespoon Dijon mustard

1 garlic clove, crushed and peeled

Kosher salt

¼ cup extra-virgin olive oil

1 large bunch curly kale, leaves stripped from the stems, washed, spun dry, cut into thin ribbons

2 ripe avocados, peeled, sliced

½ cup pistachios, toasted, coarsely chopped

This was a favorite salad at my restaurant Felidia, one that Chef Fortunato Nicotra would always make. It was one of our best-selling salads, and it became part of our family meals at home. My grandkids love it. The soft texture of the avocado and the crunchy nuts create a playful medley in your mouth. My granddaughter Olivia made this salad her own, and often makes it for herself. She gives the kale a good massage before she tosses the salad.

Halve the eggs. Coarsely chop the whites and set them aside. Put the yolks in a mini–food processor, and add the vinegar, mustard, garlic, and ½ teaspoon salt. Pulse to make a paste. With the processor running, add the olive oil in a slow, steady stream to make a smooth, thick dressing.

Put the kale in a large serving bowl. Drizzle it with a couple tablespoons of the dressing, season with ½ teaspoon salt, and massage with your hands for a minute or so, to wilt the leaves slightly. Let the kale rest for 15 minutes.

Add the egg whites, avocados, and pistachios. Toss well, and serve.

Chopped Frisée Salad with Salami and Boiled Eggs

Insalata Riccia con Salame e Uova Sode

Serves 4

⅓ cup red wine vinegar

2 teaspoons Dijon mustard

Kosher salt

⅓ cup extra-virgin olive oil

One 15.5-ounce can chickpeas, rinsed and drained

1 small red onion, finely chopped

4 ounces salami, thickly sliced, diced

4 ounces mild provola, diced

1 cup drained giardiniera, chopped

2 large heads frisée, trimmed, torn into bite-sized pieces (about 10 cups)

2 eggs, hard-boiled, quartered

I have been running restaurants since 1971—more than fifty years—and this menu item has lasted all that time. I personally enjoy eggs in almost any salad as an accompaniment. This recipe works as a side salad, an appetizer, a lunch, or a dinner. It is great at buffet tables, too. You get all of the antipasto ingredients in a single forkful.

Whisk the vinegar and mustard together in a large salad bowl, and season with 1 teaspoon salt. Whisk in the olive oil to make a smooth dressing.

Add the chickpeas, onion, salami, provola, and giardiniera, and toss to coat everything with the dressing. Add the frisée and eggs, and toss gently to combine. Season with salt, if needed, and serve.

Red Cabbage Salad with Cubed Crispy Ham

Insalata di Cavolo Cappuccio Rosso con Cubetti di Prosciutto Cotto Croccante

Serves 4 to 6

¼ cup extra-virgin olive oil

8 ounces boneless ham, julienned

1 medium red onion, chopped

Kosher salt and freshly ground black pepper

½ cup red wine vinegar

1 small head red cabbage, finely shredded (on a mandoline if you have one)

3 stalks celery, chopped

1 Granny Smith apple, peel left on, cored, cut into matchsticks

Today, hydroponic farms give us crispy greens for salad year-round, but I recall salads made from the cabbage family in the winter because that's all we had. Especially delicious is a salad of shredded red cabbage. The secret is to shave it thinly with a mandoline, or, as my grandfather would do it, slowly with a thin sharp knife, the cabbage sliced as thin as hair. As soon as the cabbage was cut, Nonna Rosa tossed it with a splash of wine vinegar, and the acidity of the vinegar kept the red brightness of the cabbage until it was ready to dress. Olive oil and vinegar, with salt and pepper, were the usual dressing, but sometimes she made a warm dressing, with some cubed ham or prosciutto crisped in olive oil with a bit of wine vinegar, brought to a boil, and tossed hot into the cut cabbage. Delicious.

Heat 2 tablespoons of the olive oil in a large skillet over medium heat. Add the ham, and cook, tossing occasionally, until it is crisp on the edges, about 3 minutes. Add the red onion, and cook just until it begins to wilt, about 2 minutes. Season lightly with salt and pepper, and whisk in the vinegar and remaining 2 tablespoons olive oil.

Combine the cabbage, celery, and apple in a large serving bowl. Pour the contents of the skillet over the cabbage, and toss well to wilt the cabbage slightly. Season with 1 teaspoon salt and several grinds of pepper. Serve warm or at room temperature.

The table ready for the Christmas Eve meal at my house, 2020

SOUPS

My whole family loves soups—and I love cooking them. A stock made of capon or free-range chicken is a holiday must, especially at the Christmas meal. Everybody's favorite is tortellini in this soup, but Farina Gnocchi (page 56) is a close second. When my mother was alive and lived with me, I made a pot of soup just about every week. I would always include some sausages, smoked pork ribs, or other cured meats so she had some protein. I put the surplus in quart containers, labeled them, and froze them. Since I worked late hours at the restaurant, my mother could defrost a container of soup and have it with a piece of Grana Padano, her favorite cheese, and some crusty Italian bread for her dinner.

———————————————

Cream of Fava Soup with Rice   45

Pasta and Pea Soup   46

Corn and Bean Soup with Kielbasa   49

Mixed Meat Broth   50

Shredded Meat Salad   51

Farro and Bean Soup with Mushrooms   52

Zucchini Soup with Eggs and Cheese   53

Tomato Soup with Fregola and Clams   55

Farina Gnocchi   56

Ricotta Soup   57

Cream of Fava Soup with Rice

Vellutata di Fave con Riso

Makes about 3 quarts

1 pound peeled dried favas,
soaked for at least 3 hours
and up to overnight

⅓ cup extra-virgin olive oil,
plus more for drizzling

8 ounces prosciutto cotto,
thickly sliced, cubed

4 garlic cloves, crushed and peeled

1 large onion, chopped

2 large carrots, chopped

2 tablespoons tomato paste

1 tablespoon chopped fresh thyme

2 fresh bay leaves

¼ teaspoon peperoncino flakes

1 cup long-grain white rice

Mostly, one thinks of favas as the puffy green pod with the fava bean in it. Well, just as all beans get dried and saved for off-season cooking, so do favas. Shelled and dried, they behave like dried peas when cooked, disintegrating and making a delicious and dense soup. When I was a little girl, it was part of my job to help Nonna Rosa pull the beans out of the pods and lay them on mats for drying so she could make rich winter soups. In my own kitchen, this was a job my mother, Erminia, took very seriously, and she would patiently sit at our kitchen table for hours, pulling beans out of pods, sometimes singing an old Italian song as she proceeded. Since the favas you use here are peeled and split before drying, you do not have to soak them as long as other dried beans—3 hours is fine. You can soak them overnight if you prefer; just be aware that the cooking time on the soup will be a little less. You can make this soup ahead, but add rice only to the portion you want to serve right away.

Drain the soaked favas and rinse them. Heat a large Dutch oven over medium heat, and add the olive oil. When the oil is hot, add the prosciutto cotto, and cook until it begins to crisp on the edges, about 3 minutes. Add the garlic, onion, and carrots, and cook until the onion begins to wilt, 5 to 6 minutes.

Make a space in the pan, and add the tomato paste to that spot. Cook and stir the tomato paste there for a minute, until it darkens a shade or two, sprinkle in the thyme, then stir this into the vegetables. Add the favas and 4 quarts water. Bring it to a simmer, and add the bay leaves and peperoncino. Bring to a rapid simmer, and cook until the favas are cooked through and have begun to fall apart, about 1½ hours.

Add the rice, return to a simmer, and cook until the rice is al dente, 14 to 16 minutes. Discard the bay leaves. Season with salt, if needed. Serve with a drizzle of olive oil.

Pasta and Pea Soup

Pasta e Bisi

Serves 8, with leftovers

Kosher salt

1½ pounds shelled fresh
peas or frozen peas

2 tablespoons extra-virgin olive oil

2 tablespoons unsalted butter

3 leeks, white and light-green parts,
halved vertically, sliced (or 1½ cups
chopped spring onions in season)

3 inner stalks celery, diced

3 garlic cloves, crushed and peeled

1 tablespoon fresh thyme
leaves, chopped

2 fresh bay leaves

¼ teaspoon peperoncino flakes

2 pieces Grana Padano rind

8 ounces ditalini or other
small pasta shape

Grana Padano, freshly
grated, for serving

This is a pasta rendition of the ever-popular risi-e-bisi soup from northeastern Italy, where my family comes from. It is best and sweetest when the peas are young and fresh, but today you can make it at any time of the year with frozen peas, always available and delicious. It's a quick and light soup, perfect for spring. When I was growing up, Nonna Rosa had peas in her garden, and I would pick and shell them for her. She would boil the pea shells, season the water with salt, and use that to make the soup, but if you don't have peas in the pod, you can just use water, as I do here. I use ditalini in this recipe, but you can certainly revert to rice to make the classic risi e bisi, though the rice might take a few minutes longer to cook.

Bring a large saucepan of salted water to a boil. Add half of the peas, and cook until very tender, 7 to 8 minutes for frozen peas, 10 for fresh. Drain, and cool under running water. Transfer them to a blender or food processor. Purée them until smooth (you can add a little water, if needed, to get things going). Set them aside.

Heat the olive oil and butter in a large Dutch oven over medium heat. When the butter is melted, add the leeks, celery, and garlic. Cook, stirring occasionally, until the leeks are wilted, 7 to 8 minutes. Add the thyme and bay leaves. Pour in 3 quarts cold water and the pea purée, and season with 1 tablespoon salt and the peperoncino. Add the cheese rinds. Bring the water to a simmer, and cook to blend the flavors and reduce by about a quarter, 15 to 20 minutes.

Add the remaining peas, and continue to simmer until they're very tender and the soup is flavorful, 25 to 35 minutes. (The soup will still be brothy at this point; it will thicken up once you add the pasta.)

Add the pasta, and simmer until it is quite al dente (it will continue to cook off heat). Discard the bay leaves. Serve with grated Grana Padano for sprinkling.

Corn and Bean Soup with Kielbasa

Zuppa di Bobici e Fagioli con Salsiccia Kielbasa

Serves 8, with leftovers

1 pound dried kidney beans

¼ cup extra-virgin olive oil

1 large onion, chopped

2 large garlic cloves, chopped

2 tablespoons tomato paste

4 medium russet potatoes, peeled (about 2½ pounds)

4 fresh bay leaves

½ teaspoon peperoncino flakes

1½ pounds kielbasa, cut into 4 segments

4 ears corn, shucked, kernels removed, cobs reserved

Kosher salt

In the Istrian dialect, we called this soup *bobici,* after the word for corn kernels. Growing up, I certainly ate enough bean-based soups, especially in the winter, "pasta e fagioli" being a meal we had once or twice a week. When spring came and the corn formed young ears, the present recipe was the soup of choice. The corn was sweet and crackled under our teeth, and it remains one of my brother, Franco's favorite soups. Grandma always added cured pork meat to enhance the flavor, and this turned the soup into a delicious two-course meal.

Pick over the beans for debris, place them in a large bowl, and add water to cover. Soak overnight in the refrigerator.

The next day, drain and rinse the beans.

In a large Dutch oven, heat the olive oil over medium heat. Add the onion and garlic, and cook, stirring occasionally, until the onion is wilted, about 5 minutes. Make a space in the pan, and add the tomato paste to that spot. Cook and stir the tomato paste there for a minute, until it darkens a shade or two.

Add 4 quarts cold water, the beans, the potatoes, bay leaves, and peperoncino. Bring the water to a simmer over medium-low heat, set the lid ajar, and simmer until the beans are almost tender, about 1 hour.

Fish out the potatoes, and place them in a bowl. Mash them with a fork, and return them to the pot. Add the kielbasa, corn, and corn cobs, and simmer until the beans are tender and the soup is thick and flavorful, 30 to 40 minutes more. Remove the bay leaves and corn cobs, and season the soup to taste with salt, depending on how salty the kielbasa is. The kielbasa can be cut into small pieces and served in the soup, or can be served separately, after the soup, with a salad or a vegetable.

Mixed Meat Broth

Brodo di Carne Mista

Makes about 4 quarts broth, plus about 2 to 3 cups cooked meat

2 pounds bone-in beef short ribs or bone-in chuck roast

1½-pound piece bone-in veal shoulder, shank, or other stewing cut

1 pound chicken necks, backs, or wings

1 large onion, halved

3 large carrots, halved crosswise

3 stalks celery, each cut into 4 pieces crosswise

6 garlic cloves, crushed and peeled

6 sprigs fresh Italian parsley

10 black peppercorns

2 or 3 pieces Grana Padano rind, scraped, washed

Kosher salt

This recipe will serve you twice—you can add rice or pasta or a grain to the broth for a quick and flavorful soup, and the shredded meat from the bones is a delicious base for a quick but hearty salad (recipe follows). If freezing, let the soup cool and then put it in pint containers, dating the lid with a marker, and then place in the freezer.

There is not a holiday without soup on our table. All generations love it. For the holidays, I usually make a clear meat broth. You can use chicken, turkey, or beef in this soup, but capon soup is a special treat usually reserved for holiday meals. When Nonna Rosa used to make this for special occasions, the pasta in the soup—if there was time to hand-make it—was anolini (page 97), small rounds filled with meat or cheese. Or sometimes she would make gnocchetti di gris (page 56), small gnocchi made out of semolina. Sometimes, after making fresh pasta for this soup, Nonna Rosa would take the leftover corner pieces of dough and cut them into little squares, quadrucci (page 97).

Wash the beef, veal, and chicken under cold running water, and drain them well. Add them to a large Dutch oven or stockpot, cover with 6 quarts cold water, and bring the water to a boil over high heat. Once the water boils, reduce the heat so it is just simmering. Simmer for 1 hour, occasionally skimming off any foam or fat that rises to the surface.

After an hour, add the onion, carrots, celery, garlic, parsley, peppercorns, and cheese rinds. Return to a simmer. Set the lid ajar, and cook until the meat is very tender, 2 to 3 hours.

Line a colander with a dampened kitchen towel or cheesecloth, and strain the broth, reserving the meat. Season the broth with 1 tablespoon salt. If you have a defatting cup, defat the broth now. Otherwise, chill the stock, and remove the fat once it solidifies. Portion and freeze the soup as directed above. Strip any usable meat from the bones and shred it; you should get about 2 to 3 cups, to use in a salad, such as the following.

Shredded Meat Salad

2 to 3 cups leftover shredded
soup meat, warm

1 small red onion, sliced

1 cup cornichons, sliced or chopped

¼ cup chopped fresh Italian parsley

2 tablespoons red wine vinegar

2 tablespoons extra-virgin olive oil

½ teaspoon kosher salt

¼ teaspoon peperoncino flakes

Toss the warm meat in a medium bowl with the red onion, cornichons, parsley, vinegar, olive oil, salt, and peperoncino, and serve warm or at room temperature.

Farro and Bean Soup with Mushrooms

Zuppa di Fagioli e Farro

Serves 8, with leftovers

1 pound dried borlotti
or cranberry beans

2 ham hocks (about 2 pounds total)

¼ cup extra-virgin olive oil,
plus more for drizzling

1 large onion, chopped

5 garlic cloves, chopped

3 tablespoons tomato paste

4 fresh bay leaves

3 medium russet potatoes, peeled

2 large carrots, chopped

¼ teaspoon peperoncino flakes

Kosher salt

1 pound mixed mushrooms
(such as button, cremini,
oyster, shiitake), sliced

1½ cups farro, rinsed, drained

This soup reminds me of the damp forest in the fall in Istria, where I grew up. You could smell the wild mushrooms growing, and we would forage for them to eat with the beans we had conserved and dried in the spring and summer. Eating this soup, I remember the fowl hunters, including my grandfather Giovanni, all bundled up for cooler weather, coming back to the table anticipating this gut-warming soup. The recipe can make a two-course meal: first serve the soup, then the ham hock with a salad, and you are all set. It is a soup that freezes well, and can be saved for those days when you need to put a quick meal on the table.

Pick over the beans for debris, place them in a large bowl, and add water to cover. Soak overnight in the refrigerator.

The next day, drain and rinse the beans. Put the ham hocks in a saucepan with water to cover, and bring the water to a simmer. Simmer for 20 minutes to remove some of the saltiness, drain, and rinse well.

In a large Dutch oven, heat the olive oil over medium heat. Add the onion and garlic, and cook, stirring occasionally, until the onion is wilted, about 5 minutes. Make a space in the pan, and add the tomato paste to that spot. Cook and stir the tomato paste there for a minute, until it darkens a shade or two.

Add 5 quarts of water, and bring it to a simmer. Add the drained beans, ham hocks, bay leaves, potatoes, carrots, and peperoncino. Simmer rapidly until the beans are tender but not falling apart and the soup is reduced by about a third, about 1 hour.

Fish out the potatoes, and place them in a bowl. Mash them with a fork, and return them to the pot. Season with 1 tablespoon salt, and add the mushrooms and farro. Simmer until the farro is just tender, about 30 to 45 minutes (cooking time can vary quite a bit for different brands of farro, so check early and often). Remove the bay leaves and ham hocks. Serve the soup with a drizzle of olive oil, and the ham hocks separately, alongside or as a separate course.

Zucchini Soup with Eggs and Cheese

Minestra di Zucchine con Uova e Formaggio

Serves 6 to 8

⅓ cup extra-virgin olive oil

1½ pounds medium zucchini, thinly sliced into half-moons

1 large onion, chopped

Kosher salt

½ teaspoon peperoncino flakes

2 fresh bay leaves

3 large eggs

½ cup freshly grated Grana Padano

¼ cup fresh basil leaves, chopped

This is one of those easy Italian soups that can be made with almost any vegetable that's in season and fortified with some grated cheese and eggs to become a whole meal. In Italy, a similar soup, stracciatella, is served to young children as a full meal containing vegetable, protein, and dairy. This is my version, which I served to my grandkids when they were little. I fondly remember tying kitchen towels around their necks to use as bibs and letting them feed themselves, hoping more made it into their mouths than onto the towels.

Heat the olive oil in a large Dutch oven over medium-low heat. When the oil is hot, add the zucchini and onion. Cook, stirring occasionally, until the vegetables begin to soften, 8 to 10 minutes. Season with 2 teaspoons salt and the peperoncino. Add 2 quarts water and the bay leaves, and bring to a vigorous simmer. Cook until the zucchini is very tender but not falling apart, about 30 minutes.

Meanwhile, beat the eggs in a bowl with ½ teaspoon salt, the cheese, and the basil until well combined. Slowly pour the egg mixture into the soup, stirring as you go, to make shreds of egg. Once all of the egg mixture has been incorporated, return the soup to a simmer briefly, then remove it from the heat, discard the bay leaves, and let the soup stand 5 minutes before serving.

Tomato Soup with Fregola and Clams

Zuppa di Pomodoro con Fregola e Vongole

Serves 4 to 6

6 tablespoons extra-virgin olive oil, plus more for drizzling

4 garlic cloves, crushed and peeled, plus 3 garlic cloves, thinly sliced

2 teaspoons chopped fresh thyme

One 28-ounce can whole San Marzano tomatoes, crushed by hand

Kosher salt

½ teaspoon peperoncino flakes

1 cup dry white wine

3 pounds Manila or small littleneck clams

1 pound fregola

¼ cup chopped fresh Italian parsley

There is not one person in my family who does not adore clams, and we eat them in a variety of ways. Stuffed clams are great for an appetizer; a big pot of clams sautéed with some onions and seasonings can make a whole meal as you pick through, enjoying the juices and slurping down the clams. As a young girl, I would go to the sea and collect clams, mostly cockles and smaller clams than what are seen in America today. This soup has also become one of our family's favorite ways to enjoy clams. Tomato soup is a popular soup in America, but here is an Italian rendition that can be a main course. Though I have added clams, it can be made with mussels, shrimps, scallops, or even mixed seafood; just mind the cooking time that each requires. Fregola comes in different sizes. I use large ones here, but if yours are smaller, start checking for doneness after 10 minutes.

You can leave a few clams in their shells for an attractive presentation, as I do here, or remove them all.

Heat 3 tablespoons of the olive oil in a large Dutch oven over medium heat. When the oil is hot, add the crushed garlic and thyme, and cook until the garlic is sizzling, about 1 minute. Add the tomatoes and 2 quarts water. Season with 2 teaspoons salt and the peperoncino. Bring to a simmer, and cook until slightly thickened, about 15 minutes.

Meanwhile, heat another Dutch oven or pot over medium heat. Add the remaining 3 tablespoons olive oil. When the oil is hot, add the sliced garlic, let it sizzle for a minute, and then pour in the white wine. Bring it to a simmer, and add the clams. Cover, and cook until the clams open, about 5 minutes; discard any that do not. Remove the clams to a large bowl with a spider strainer, and strain the cooking liquid over the top. Let it cool. Pluck the clams from their shells, and leave them in the liquid, discarding the shells.

Once the tomato mixture has thickened, add the fregola and cook until it's al dente, about 20 minutes. Stir in the clams and their liquid, and the parsley. Simmer to heat the clams through and bring all the flavors together, about 2 minutes. Serve with a drizzle of olive oil.

Farina Gnocchi

Gnocchetti di Gris

Serves 6

12 cups low-sodium or homemade chicken stock

1 large egg

2 tablespoons unsalted butter, at room temperature

½ teaspoon kosher salt

½ cup farina cereal, such as Cream of Wheat (don't use instant), plus more as needed

Grana Padano, freshly grated, for serving

My mother, Grandma Erminia, was the expert maker of gnocchetti di gris. I would be busy in the kitchen, prepping all the vegetables for the soup and at the stove pulling it together, while she would sit at the kitchen table with a bowl between her knees, mixing the egg, cheese, and farina flour and deftly shaping the mixture into gnocchetti, her hands moving at the speed of light. The process for her was pure muscle memory; she had made them her whole life. It was a pleasure to watch.

I now make the gnocchetti di gris myself. They are easy, and all you need is a good stock or soup to cook them in. I sometimes cook them like pasta, in boiling salted water. When they boil up and are tender, I fish them out with a spider strainer, set them in a bowl, cover them with plastic wrap, and add them to the hot stock to reheat and serve.

Heat 6 cups of the stock in a large saucepan over medium heat so it is simmering lightly.

Combine the egg, butter, and salt in a medium bowl, and beat with a fork to combine well. Add the farina, and mix and mash well to make a smooth, thick dough with no lumps of butter. (If the dough doesn't hold together, add another sprinkle of farina and mix again.)

Dip a teaspoon in water, and use it to scoop a spoonful of dough. Use another spoon to scoop the dough off into the simmering stock. Repeat with the remaining dough, wetting the spoons as needed to keep the gnocchetti from sticking. Return the stock to a simmer. Cover, and simmer gently, stirring occasionally, until the gnocchetti have expanded and are cooked through, about 30 minutes. Remove the pan from the heat and let it rest for 15 minutes.

Heat the remaining 6 cups stock in another saucepan. Remove the gnocchi to the new stock with a slotted spoon. Skim the first pot of stock to remove any foam or fat, and pour it through a strainer into the second pot. Return all to a simmer.

Serve in bowls, with a sprinkle of grated cheese.

Ricotta Soup

Minestra di Ricotta

Serves 6

Kosher salt

1 pound fresh pasta dough
(page 97)

All-purpose flour, for dusting

2 cups (1 pound) good-
quality fresh ricotta

¼ cup extra-virgin olive oil

1 cup fresh basil leaves, shredded

Kosher salt and freshly
ground black pepper

½ cup freshly grated pecorino

Ricotta was often produced in the courtyard of my childhood home. It was easy to make from the abundant goat milk we had and could be eaten or used right away, as opposed to aged cheeses, which needed more time and work, so we used it in many recipes. Often, it simply topped a piece of bread with a drizzle of our honey on top. Mixing fresh ricotta into a pasta sauce is quite common, but in this recipe the ricotta actually becomes a dressing for freshly cooked pasta. It is light and delicious, something between a soup and a pasta dish.

Bring a large pot of salted water to a boil for the pasta.

Roll the pasta dough on a floured work surface, as detailed on page 98. Cut into 8-by-1-by-3-inch ribbons of pappardelle. Dust them with flour, slowly turning the pasta strands, twist them to form into nests, and set them aside while you prepare the dressing.

In a large serving bowl, combine the ricotta, olive oil, basil, 1 teaspoon salt, and several grinds of pepper.

Add the pasta to the boiling water. Ladle 1½ cups of the pasta-cooking water into the ricotta mixture, and stir well to combine.

When the pasta is al dente, remove it with tongs or a wire strainer to the bowl, without draining it too much—let the water dripping from the pasta go into the bowl as well. Sprinkle with the pecorino, and toss to combine. Serve immediately.

Antipasto spread before the Christmas meal at my house, 2020

VEGETABLES AND SIDES

We Italians love our vegetables, and we serve them at every meal, but today, more than ever, I find that vegetables can become a whole meal. With the addition of some cheese, legumes, or boiled eggs or potatoes to the vegetables or salad, a meal is created. Grandma Erminia loved her garden and everything that came from it. She would make a whole meal out of boiled potatoes or boiled eggs with her salads and greens.

———————————————

Asparagus with Lemon Sauce   62

Fennel with Anchovies and Olives   63

Stewed Eggplant and Peppers   65

Rosemary Chickpeas   66

Crispy Baked Zucchini, Carrots, and Cherry Tomatoes   67

Butternut Squash and Cannellini Beans   68

Corn and Greens with Prosciutto Cotto   70

Onion and Potato Gratin   71

Smashed Garlic Rosemary Potatoes   73

Roasted Celery, Carrots, and Onions   74

Braised Cabbage with Onion and Garlic   75

Roasted Spaghetti Squash with Spicy Tomato Sauce   76

Cider-Roasted Apples   78

Roasted Onion Salad   79

Fava Beans with Mint   81

Asparagus with Lemon Sauce

Asparagi con Salsa al Limone

Serves 4 to 6

Kosher salt

2 bunches medium asparagus,
tough ends removed,
lower stalks peeled

2 eggs, hard-boiled,
whites and yolks separated

Juice and zest of 1 lemon

Freshly ground black pepper

⅓ cup extra-virgin olive oil

3 tablespoons capers in brine,
drained

Asparagus and eggs were both abundant in my childhood—the chickens and ducks gave us eggs, and the asparagus was foraged wild in the spring. When I was growing up, we didn't have a freezer or an icebox, so the asparagus was eaten only in season. Now, every March, I go back to Istria to forage for wild asparagus and eat my fill, as much as I can, every day. Besides eating my fill of wild asparagus, it is a nostalgic return to my childhood and the places I cherish. The extra I have foraged, I freeze in small bunches so the pleasure can last me a little bit longer throughout the year. Asparagus and eggs is a combination I have been eating for as long as I can remember. Asparagus-and-egg frittata, asparagus-and-egg salad—and now this flavorful, simple preparation is one of my favorite ways to serve asparagus.

Bring a large pot of salted water to a boil, and set up a large bowl with ice water next to the stove. Add the asparagus to the boiling water. Cook until just tender, 3 to 5 minutes. Transfer to the ice bath, and let it chill completely.

For the dressing, combine the egg yolks, lemon juice, ½ teaspoon salt, and several grinds of pepper in a mini–food processor. Pulse until smooth. With the processor running, add the olive oil in a slow stream to make a creamy, smooth dressing. Stir in the capers. Finely chop the egg whites and place them in a small bowl. Add the lemon zest, and toss well to combine.

Pat the chilled asparagus dry, and arrange it on a serving platter. Spoon the dressing over the top. Sprinkle with the egg whites, and serve.

Fennel with Anchovies and Olives

Finocchio con Acciughe e Olive

Serves 4 to 6

¼ cup extra-virgin olive oil

3 large fennel bulbs, trimmed, cored, cut into 1-inch chunks

1 large onion, cut into 1-inch chunks

Kosher salt

½ teaspoon peperoncino flakes

6 anchovies packed in oil, drained, chopped

1 cup pitted Cerignola olives, halved

Fishing is a favorite pastime of mine. I fished as a young girl with my uncle Emilio, and now I love taking my grandkids on fishing vacations. I would go after little fish with a net when I was young, but now we reel in the big fish, especially when I'm fishing with Miles and Ethan—their youthful strength is helpful. On one of our fishing trips to Alaska, Miles reeled in a 25-pound halibut. Our guide filleted the fish, and we shipped it to New York to be shared with the family. Little fish like fresh anchovies or sardines, my favorite fishes, we often pan-fried and ate between two pieces of bread, like a sandwich, or just popped into our mouths. In this recipe, the cured anchovies are sautéed and complement the mellow licorice flavor of the fennel. This preparation of fennel is a great vegetable side for roasted or grilled meats as well as fish, but if you chop the ingredients finer, it can also be a sauce for pasta or a topping for bruschetta.

Heat a large skillet over medium heat. Add the olive oil. When the oil is hot, add the fennel and onion, and cook until everything just begins to wilt, about 5 minutes. Season with 1 teaspoon salt and the peperoncino, and add ½ cup water. Bring to a simmer, cover, and cook until just tender, about 15 minutes.

Uncover, and add the anchovies and olives. Cook, stirring often, over medium-low heat until the liquid is reduced away and the fennel and onions are caramelized and very tender, about 15 minutes more.

Stewed Eggplant and Peppers

Melanzane e Peperoni Stufati

Serves 4 to 6

2 medium Italian eggplants (totaling about 1½ pounds)

¼ cup extra-virgin olive oil

1 medium sweet onion, coarsely chopped

2 garlic cloves, crushed and peeled

1 red bell pepper, seeded, thickly sliced

1 yellow bell pepper, seeded, cut into 1-inch pieces

Kosher salt

Peperoncino flakes

¼ cup tomato paste

¼ cup red wine vinegar

6 tablespoons capers in brine, drained

¼ cup chopped fresh basil

Caponata is a delicious traditional Sicilian mélange of summer vegetables. This dish is for when you want caponata but don't have all the ingredients. My son-in-law, Corrado, is particularly fond of eggplant and will eat it in any preparation, especially eggplant parmigiana, which he has grown quite adept at making. Being a Roman, though, he really appreciates some of the more traditionally southern-Italian dishes I make, like this one. A great vegetable dish, it can be a side dish, or it can be a breakfast-brunch dish—just poach a few eggs and put them on top. You can even turn it into a risotto or a pasta dish topped with some ricotta.

Remove vertical strips of peel from the eggplant with a vegetable peeler, and cut the flesh into 1-to-2-inch cubes.

Heat the olive oil in a large skillet over medium heat. Add the onion, and cook until it begins to soften, 2 to 3 minutes. Add the garlic and eggplant, and toss to coat them in the oil. Cover the skillet, and let everything sweat until the eggplant begins to soften, about 4 minutes. Uncover, and add the peppers. Season with 1 teaspoon salt and a big pinch of peperoncino. Cover, and let sweat, stirring occasionally, until the vegetables are just cooked through, about 10 minutes.

Meanwhile, combine the tomato paste, vinegar, and ¾ cup water in a spouted measuring cup, and whisk to combine. Once the vegetables are cooked through, add the vinegar mixture and capers, and cover the skillet again. Cook until the vegetables are meltingly soft, 5 to 10 minutes more.

Uncover the skillet, and increase the heat to reduce the sauce slightly, 1 to 2 minutes. Season with salt if needed. Stir in the basil.

Rosemary Chickpeas

Ceci al Rosmarino

Serves 6 to 8

1 pound dried chickpeas,
soaked overnight

2 medium carrots,
cut into ½-inch chunks

4 fresh bay leaves

¼ cup plus 2 tablespoons
extra-virgin olive oil

Kosher salt

4 garlic cloves, thinly sliced

1 bunch scallions, chopped,
white and green parts separated

1 tablespoon fresh rosemary
leaves, chopped

½ teaspoon peperoncino flakes

When I was growing up, we always had dried beans and hedges of rosemary, huge hedges that I used to love to run through. I'd come out smelling like a bouquet of rosemary. Even today, I have quite a few rosemary bushes and go to them for my cooking needs. The aroma brings back many childhood memories. This is a great vegetarian main dish, flavorful and very economical. Add some water and cook some pasta in the chickpeas, and they become more complex, perfect for a vegetarian main course. As is, it's a good side dish for meats like grilled lamb or pork chops. It keeps well in the fridge for a week.

Drain and rinse the soaked chickpeas. Add to a pot with water to cover by about an inch. Add the carrots, bay leaves, and 2 tablespoons of the olive oil. Bring to a simmer, cover, and cook until the chickpeas are almost tender, 40 minutes to 1 hour. Uncover, and simmer until the chickpeas are tender all the way through, 20 to 30 minutes more. Discard the bay leaves, and season with 2 teaspoons salt.

Heat a large skillet over medium heat. Add the remaining ¼ cup olive oil and the garlic, scallion whites, rosemary, and peperoncino. Cook until everything is sizzling, about 1 minute. Carefully add the chickpeas and carrots in their liquid to the skillet. Bring the liquid to a simmer, and cook to blend the flavors, about 10 minutes. Use a potato masher to mash the chickpeas slightly, to thicken the sauce. Stir in the scallion greens. Season with salt, if needed, and serve.

Crispy Baked Zucchini, Carrots, and Cherry Tomatoes

Zucchine Croccanti al Forno con Carote e Pomodorini

Serves 6

3 medium zucchini, cut into ½-inch half-moons

1 pint cherry or grape tomatoes, halved

4 rainbow carrots, sliced ½ inch thick on the bias

3 tablespoons extra-virgin olive oil

Kosher salt

1 cup freshly grated Grana Padano or pecorino

1 teaspoon sweet paprika

For the past forty years, I have grown small cherry tomatoes in my home garden. As I garden, I love to pop a few small tomatoes into my mouth; however, my favorite memory is of the tiny fingers of my grandchildren, when they were babies, toddling through the garden, just about as tall as the tomato plants were high, picking and eating the sweet tomatoes. Roasting those tomatoes and other vegetables heightens the sweetness, and intensifies all the flavors. This recipe is summer vegetables made easy in the oven. It's a great side dish for any meat or fish, or just crack some eggs on top of the vegetables in the pan toward the end to make a complete meal.

Preheat the oven to 425 degrees.

Combine the zucchini, tomatoes, and carrots in a large oval gratin dish or rimmed half sheet pan. Drizzle with the olive oil. Toss well. Season with 1 teaspoon salt, and toss again. Cover with foil, and roast until the carrots and zucchini are almost tender and the cherry tomatoes have wilted, about 20 minutes.

Combine the grated cheese and paprika in a small bowl. Sprinkle this evenly over the vegetables. (If using a sheet pan, first push the vegetables in one layer toward the center of the pan so there is not too much space in between the pieces.) Roast again until the cheese forms a crispy crust, 15 to 20 minutes more. Serve warm.

Butternut Squash and Cannellini Beans

Zucca con Fagioli Cannellini

Serves 6

FOR THE BALSAMIC REDUCTION

1 cup balsamic vinegar

1 tablespoon honey

1 fresh bay leaf

1 sprig fresh rosemary

FOR THE SQUASH AND BEANS

⅓ cup extra-virgin olive oil, plus more for drizzling

1 medium butternut squash, peeled, cubed

Kosher salt

Peperoncino flakes

4 garlic cloves, crushed and peeled

3 fresh bay leaves

2 cups cooked cannellini beans (or one 15.5-ounce can, rinsed and drained)

3 scallions, chopped

Beans are great by themselves as well as being an excellent complement to vegetables or proteins. I like these kinds of side dishes because in one pot you have the legumes and the vegetables. Here the beans and squash are sweet; the tartness and complexity of the balsamic reduction balances them out. I usually toast up two slices of bread and use them to accompany this dish and to sop up any juices.

For the balsamic reduction: Combine the balsamic, honey, bay leaf, and rosemary in a small saucepan or skillet. Bring to a boil, and cook until it's syrupy, 4 to 5 minutes. (Watch carefully toward the end, so it doesn't scorch.) Remove and discard the rosemary and bay leaf. Let the mixture cool. You should have about 3 to 4 tablespoons syrupy balsamic reduction.

For the squash and beans: Heat a large skillet over medium heat. Add the olive oil. When the oil is hot, add the butternut squash, and toss to coat it in the oil. Season with 1 teaspoon salt and a big pinch of peperoncino. Cook to brown the edges of the squash, about 4 minutes; then add the garlic and bay leaves and 1 cup water. Reduce the heat so the mixture is simmering. Cover, and cook until the squash is almost tender, about 15 minutes more, stirring occasionally.

Uncover, and add the beans and scallions. Cook until the scallions wilt and the beans are heated through, 3 to 4 minutes. Discard the bay leaves. Season with salt, if needed, and add a final drizzle of olive oil. Serve in the skillet or a shallow serving bowl. Drizzle with some of the balsamic reduction at the table. (If you don't use all of the reduction, it will keep at room temperature in a small covered container for a week, and you can use it to finish vegetables, fish, pork, or chicken.)

Corn and Greens with Prosciutto Cotto

Mais e Verdure con Prosciutto Cotto

Serves 4 to 6

¼ cup extra-virgin olive oil

2 ounces prosciutto cotto or ham, thickly sliced, chopped

1 small bunch each kale and Swiss chard, stemmed (reserve the tender chard stems), leaves roughly chopped

1 teaspoon kosher salt

¼ teaspoon peperoncino flakes

4 scallions, chopped

4 ears corn, kernels removed

1 small bunch spinach, stemmed, leaves roughly chopped

Everyone loves a quick vegetable dish, and my grandkids, who are young adults now, often ask my advice on what to make. They usually don't have much time to shop and are looking to use what is in the refrigerator, so this recipe is perfect. Most people have leafy greens on hand, and you can even substitute canned corn if you don't have fresh. Verdure strascinate is a common Italian way of preparing greens; it literally means "dragged vegetables." Here I add some prosciutto cotto for protein, and some corn for sweetness, to make an easy summer meal.

Heat the olive oil in a large Dutch oven over medium heat. Add the prosciutto cotto, and cook, stirring occasionally, until the edges are crisp, about 2 minutes. Chop the chard stems, and add them to the pot. Cook and stir until the edges begin to wilt, 3 to 4 minutes. Add the chard and kale leaves. Season with 1 teaspoon salt and the peperoncino. Stir, cover, and cook until the greens are fully wilted, 5 to 7 minutes.

Add the scallions, and cook until they begin to wilt, about 2 minutes. Stir in the corn, cover, and cook until the kernels are tender, 8 to 10 minutes. Add the spinach, and cook, stirring often, until all of the greens are very tender and most of the liquid in the pan has reduced away, 3 to 5 minutes. Serve hot.

Onion and Potato Gratin

Cipolla e Patate Gratinate

Serves 8

2 tablespoons unsalted butter, plus more for the baking dish

2 large sweet onions, thickly sliced

Kosher salt

8 large fresh sage leaves

1 cup heavy cream

1 cup whole milk

2 fresh bay leaves

2 pounds medium russet potatoes, peeled, sliced about ¼ inch thick

6 ounces Italian Fontina, grated

¾ cup freshly grated Grana Padano

This is a great dish to make when I am cooking for the whole family or a large group, since it goes in the oven and doesn't require a lot of prep time or attention while it's cooking. Onions, potatoes, cream, and cheese come together here, in the ultimate side dish. This gratin is easy to put together; then just slip it into the oven, next to whatever you are roasting, and toss a salad, and your balanced meal is done. Think about this dish when you are having people over for brunch or breakfast. Make it in a large baking pan, cut it into squares, and serve each portion on a dish with a fried or poached egg or two on top.

Butter a 9-by-13-inch baking dish, and set it aside. Preheat the oven to 400 degrees.

Melt the 2 tablespoons butter in a medium Dutch oven over medium heat. When the butter is melted, add the onions, season with 1 teaspoon salt, and cook, stirring occasionally, until the onions are wilted, about 10 minutes.

Add the sage leaves, let them sizzle for a minute, then add the cream, milk, and bay leaves. Bring to a simmer, and season with 1 teaspoon salt. Add the potatoes, and simmer just to combine, 3 to 4 minutes.

Add the Fontina and Grana Padano to a medium bowl, and toss to combine them. Transfer half of the potato-and-cream mixture to the baking dish, and spread it in an even layer. Sprinkle with half of the cheese mixture. Repeat with the remaining potatoes, then the cheese. Cover the baking dish with foil, and bake until it's bubbly and the potatoes are tender, about 30 minutes. Uncover, and bake until the top is golden brown and crusty and the potatoes have absorbed the cream and are no longer soupy (it will thicken up more as it cools as well), about 30 minutes more. Discard the sage and bay leaves. Let cool for 5 to 10 minutes before serving.

Smashed Garlic Rosemary Potatoes

Patate Schiacciate con Aglio e Rosmarino

Serves 4 to 6

Kosher salt

1½ pounds small Yukon Gold potatoes (about the size of walnuts in the shell)

3 tablespoons extra-virgin olive oil

Fresh rosemary sprigs

4 large garlic cloves, thickly sliced

Everybody likes crispy potatoes, and though these require a little manual labor, they yield great results. You could also use small red potatoes, but Yukon Golds are extra creamy and delicious. Apply light but even pressure when smashing the potatoes; you want to flatten them, but you don't want them to disintegrate. This recipe reminds me of the patate in tecia my grandmother used to make in her big cast-iron pot, a simpler rendition of home fries, softer in consistency and made with nothing but potatoes, onions, and olive oil.

Preheat the oven to 450 degrees. Line a baking sheet with parchment. Put the potatoes in a large pot with salted water to cover by about 2 inches. Bring to a simmer, and cook until the potatoes are just tender, 10 to 15 minutes. Drain well.

Put the potatoes in a large bowl, drizzle with the olive oil, and season with 1 teaspoon salt. Add the rosemary and garlic, and toss well.

Pour the contents of the bowl onto the baking sheet, and use the bottom of a jar or a potato masher to bust open and flatten each potato, keeping them mostly whole.

Roast until the potatoes are very crisp and golden, about 20 to 25 minutes, and serve immediately.

Roasted Celery, Carrots, and Onions

Sedano, Carote e Cipolla Arrosto

Serves 6

6 stalks celery, peeled if tough,
cut into 2-inch pieces

3 large carrots, peeled,
cut into 2-inch pieces

2 small onions, cut into 6 wedges
each, left attached at the root end

8 sprigs fresh thyme

4 garlic cloves, crushed and peeled

5 tablespoons extra-virgin olive oil

1 teaspoon celery seeds

Kosher salt

1 cup low-sodium chicken
or vegetable stock

½ cup blanched almonds,
finely chopped

½ cup freshly grated Grana Padano

¼ cup fine dried bread crumbs

¼ cup chopped fresh Italian parsley

Roasting vegetables is the way to go, because the roasting concentrates all the sweetness and flavor of the vegetables. Be sure to season them enough to accent that sweetness. You can roast any combination of vegetables like this—just choose vegetables that all take about the same amount of time to roast. Every holiday meal features some form of roasted vegetables, but this is really the go-to recipe for our family. Sometimes, I might choose to add in a few parsnips as well. Roasted vegetables make the best accompaniment to roasted or braised meats, or chicken when done in the oven.

Preheat the oven to 425 degrees with racks in the upper and lower thirds. Spread the celery, carrots, onions, thyme, and garlic on a rimmed baking sheet or large gratin dish. Drizzle with 3 tablespoons of the olive oil, and sprinkle with the celery seeds and 1½ teaspoons salt. Toss well. Pour in the stock, cover tightly with foil, and roast on the bottom rack until the vegetables are almost tender, about 20 minutes. Uncover, and continue to roast until most of the stock has reduced away, 5 to 10 minutes more.

Meanwhile, combine the almonds, Grana Padano, bread crumbs, and parsley in a small bowl, and toss well. Drizzle the mixture with the remaining 2 tablespoons olive oil, and toss to coat. Sprinkle the crumbs over the vegetables. Move to the top rack of the oven, and roast until the crumbs are crisp and golden and the vegetables are tender and caramelized, about 20 minutes more. Serve hot.

Braised Cabbage with Onion and Garlic

Verza Stufata con Cipolla e Aglio

Serves 6

3 tablespoons extra-virgin olive oil

6-ounce piece pancetta, diced

1 large onion, sliced

4 garlic cloves, crushed and peeled

1 small head green or savoy cabbage, cored, thickly sliced

Kosher salt

¼ teaspoon peperoncino flakes

¼ cup white wine vinegar

The colder months give fewer vegetable choices, but cabbage is a favorite of mine, and, really, I eat it any time of the year. It is fabulous braised, as in this recipe, and when I cook it, I need to make a huge potful, sometimes using two heads of cabbage, to make sure there is enough for everyone. Sometimes, especially in the winter, you can find beautiful heads of cabbage, but how to prepare them beyond coleslaw? Try this simple recipe and cabbage will appear regularly on your shopping list.

Heat the oil in a large Dutch oven over medium heat. When the oil is hot, add the pancetta, and cook until it's crisped, 3 to 4 minutes. Scatter in the onion slices and garlic, and cook, stirring occasionally, until they're wilted, about 4 minutes. Add the cabbage, and toss to coat in the oil. Cook, stirring occasionally, until the cabbage starts to wilt, 4 to 5 minutes. Season with 1 teaspoon salt and the peperoncino. Add the vinegar and 1 cup water. Bring to a simmer, cover, and cook until the cabbage is very tender, 25 to 30 minutes.

Uncover, and increase the heat to reduce away excess liquid until the cabbage is nicely glazed, about 15 minutes. Serve hot.

Roasted Spaghetti Squash with Spicy Tomato Sauce

Spaghetti di Zucca con Salsa al Pomodoro Piccante

Serves 4 to 6

1 large spaghetti squash,
halved lengthwise, seeded

¼ cup extra-virgin olive oil,
plus more for brushing

Kosher salt

1 medium onion, sliced

4 hot pickled cherry peppers,
seeded, chopped

One 24-ounce jar tomato passata

1 teaspoon dried oregano,
preferably Sicilian oregano
on the branch

Peperoncino flakes

½ cup coarsely chopped fresh basil

½ cup freshly grated Grana Padano

If you are watching your carbs but are longing for spaghetti, this is the recipe you need, simple and delicious. Take care to not overbake the squash. It is done when a paring knife can be inserted with just a little resistance. When you are dressing the squash, treat it like spaghetti: toss it well, so every strand gets dressed, and do not forget the basil and the grated Grana Padano. In our family, we mainly ate squash roasted as a side dish or in a salad, or used it in the dough of fresh pasta, or as a stuffing for filled pastas. Spaghetti squash was something new for me, but it is a great alternative for anyone who is gluten-free.

Preheat the oven to 425 degrees. Line a baking sheet with parchment.

Brush the cut sides of the squash with olive oil, and season with ½ teaspoon salt. Lay the pieces, cut side down, on the baking sheet, and roast until a paring knife inserted into the center of the squash slides out with just a little resistance, 25 to 30 minutes.

While the squash roasts, make the sauce. In a large skillet, heat ¼ cup olive oil over medium heat. Add the onion, and cook until it's softened, about 4 minutes. Add the chopped peppers, and cook until they're sizzling, about 1 minute. Add the tomato passata, and bring it to a simmer. Stir in 1 cup water, the oregano, 1 teaspoon salt, and a big pinch of peperoncino. Simmer until slightly thickened, 10 to 12 minutes.

While the squash is still hot, use two forks to loosen it into strands and transfer these to the skillet with the simmering sauce. Toss with tongs to coat the strands in the sauce. Add the basil and grated cheese, toss well, and serve.

Cider-Roasted Apples

Mele Arrosto al Sidro

Serves 4 to 6

4 large Golden Delicious or other baking apples, peel left on, cored, cut into 4 wedges each

3 tablespoons unsalted butter, melted

1 cup unfiltered apple cider

½ cup white wine

Kosher salt

½ teaspoon ground ginger

½ teaspoon ground cinnamon

I love fruit with my meats, especially with roasts, but this recipe, topped with some whipped cream or ice cream, could be a dessert as well. Baked fruit is a big part of the Italian dessert repertoire, and something I ate all the time as a child. During the winter months, I still often bake quince with a bit of sugar in the core, a favorite family dessert. This recipe is a perfect side dish for the Roast Pork Shoulder on page 174. Use baking apples, such as Golden Delicious, so they'll hold their shape well during baking.

Preheat the oven to 400 degrees.

Put the apples in a 9-by-13-inch glass or ceramic baking dish. Drizzle with the melted butter. Add the cider, white wine, ½ teaspoon salt, the ginger, and the cinnamon. Stir to combine.

Roast, tossing occasionally, until the apples are tender and juicy, 20 to 25 minutes. Serve hot. (If you want the apples to be more glazed and less saucy, you can also pour the juices into a skillet to reduce them slightly, then toss again with the apples.)

Roasted Onion Salad

Insalata di Cipolle Arrosto

Serves 4

4 large Vidalia or other sweet onions, cut into ½-inch-thick rounds

⅓ cup extra-virgin olive oil

Kosher salt and freshly ground black pepper

2 tablespoons red wine vinegar

Onions often end up in salads of all kinds, but in this case they are the star. It is important that you use large, sweet onions for this salad, thickly sliced. The roasting and the dressing are the easy part; just make sure that the onions are well caramelized on both sides but still retain some texture. They should not get mushy. These roasted onions also make a great topping for a grilled steak or pork chop.

Preheat the oven to 400 degrees. Line two rimmed baking sheets with parchment, and lay the onion slices out on them so there is space between them.

In a small bowl, combine the olive oil with 1½ teaspoons salt and a generous grinding of pepper. Brush the oil onto the slices, flip them, and brush the rest on the other side. Roast until the onions are golden on the bottom, 20 to 25 minutes.

Flip the slices with a spatula, and continue to roast until very tender and caramelized, 20 to 25 minutes more.

Let them cool for a few minutes; then transfer them to a serving bowl. Drizzle with the vinegar, and toss well. Season with salt and pepper if needed, and serve them warm.

Fava Beans with Mint

Fave con la Menta

Serves 4 to 6

Kosher salt

4 pounds fava beans in the shell

2 tablespoons extra-virgin olive oil

2 ounces pancetta, thickly
sliced, cut into thin strips

2 spring onions, sliced,
or 1 small onion, chopped

Kosher salt

Peperoncino flakes

1 cup low-sodium chicken broth

¼ cup fresh mint leaves

2-ounce piece provola

Fava beans, also known as broad beans, are a spring vegetable eaten all over the world. With their cushiony pod and thick skin, they are one of the oldest beans. Preparing them is a bit of work but well worth the effort. When my grandchildren were small, I had them shell these beans, and then my mother used to sit at the table and shell them as she grew older (it was a good easy job she could do while sitting down). She lived to be a hundred, and her mobility was impaired, but she was always ready to sit at the table and help with the preparation of the vegetables. Cleaning garlic was her specialty, likewise the tedious work of shelling fresh beans, especially favas, which need a double shelling—first from the pod, then, after they're blanched, from the skin. I miss her, and now I reminisce whenever I shell them myself, waiting for the crowd to come and enjoy the dish at my table. Today, fava beans can be bought frozen; they're easier to prepare, and just as good.

Bring a large pot of salted water to a boil, and prepare a bowl with ice and water. Remove the favas from the shells. Add them to the boiling water, and bring to a boil. Blanch for 1 minute, and remove them to an ice bath. When they're cool, drain and pat them dry. Remove the outer skin. You should have about 3 cups peeled favas. (You can also use an equivalent amount of peeled frozen favas.)

Heat the olive oil in a large skillet over medium heat. Add the pancetta, and cook until the fat is rendered, about 3 minutes. Add the spring onions, and cook until they're tender, about 3 minutes. Stir in the favas, and season with ½ teaspoon salt and a big pinch of peperoncino. Add the stock, bring to a simmer, and cook until the favas are cooked through and just beginning to break down, 8 to 10 minutes.

Remove from the heat, shred the mint over the top, and gently stir it in. Grate the provola over the top, and serve immediately.

Buonavia, my first restaurant, in Forest Hills, Queens, 1971

PASTA, POLENTA, CRESPELLE, AND RISOTTO

Carbohydrates, whether in the form of pasta, rice, crespelle, or polenta, are a must every day in at least one of the meals for Italians. This tradition certainly holds true in our family. Grandma Erminia loved her pasta, especially, but it had to have a lot of cheese in it—ideally, ricotta, her favorite. She liked polenta as well. In the northeast of Italy, where we come from, we are called *polentoni*, because we eat a lot of polenta. In lean times, it filled our bellies, it was accessible, and, like pasta, it could be dressed with just about anything: fish, meat, vegetables, just sauce, or, of course, cheese, which made Grandma Erminia very happy.

———————————

Crespelle   86

Crespelle with Herb Pesto   87

Crespelle Manicotti with Spinach   89

Mushroom Ragù with Greens over Polenta   90

Risotto with Asparagus and Favas   92

Pumpkin Risotto   93

Shrimp and Tomato Risotto   94

Barley Risotto with Cabbage and Sausage   96

Fresh Pasta for Pappardelle/Tagliatelle/Quadrucci/Fuzi/Pasutice/Anolini   97

Fuzi with Chicken Ragù   100

Istrian Pasutice with Mixed Seafood   103

Pappardelle with Lamb Ragù   104

Ricotta Cavatelli with Arugula   106

Gnocchi with Sauce from Erice   108

———————————————

Sweet Potato Chickpea Gnocchi with Gorgonzola   110

Timballo with Sausage Ragù   112

Spaghetti in Lemon Cream Sauce   115

Bucatini with Broccoli Walnut Pesto   116

Spicy Lobster Linguine   117

Spaghetti with Mixed Spring Vegetables   120

Fettuccine with Caramelized Onions, Bacon, and Olives   121

Penne Rigate with Sausage, Mushrooms, and Ricotta   122

Rigatoni with Turkey Meatballs   123

Rigatoni with Sausage and Cabbage   125

Spaghetti with Roasted Cherry Tomato Sauce   126

Four-Cheese Baked Macaroni   128

Breakfast Pasta Frittata   129

———————————————

Crespelle

Makes about 20 crespelle

3 large eggs

2 cups milk

1 cup cold water,
plus more as needed

½ cup club soda, chilled

3 cups all-purpose flour

1 teaspoon kosher salt

6 tablespoons unsalted butter,
melted and cooled, plus more
melted butter for cooking the
crêpes

1 teaspoon freshly grated
lemon zest

Crespelle, Italian crêpes, are one of the most versatile recipes in the kitchen. You can use them shredded in soups, layered in lasagna, stuffed and rolled in manicotti, or baked with vegetables and pesto, and if you add some sugar to the batter, you can make endless forms of dessert with them. My favorite dessert rendition is to slather them with some rose hip jam, roll them into cigars, and eat them. I could not get enough of them in my childhood. I like to make a big batch of crespelle—once you get going, they are done in no time, and you can freeze or refrigerate the extras.

In a large bowl, combine the eggs, milk, water, and club soda, and whisk well. Add the flour and salt, and mix just to combine—don't overmix. Stir in the 6 tablespoons melted butter and lemon zest. If you're new to making crespelle, you can stop here. I like my batter a bit thinner, but the crespelle are a little harder to handle with a thin batter. As you get experienced, thin the batter out with a bit more water, a little at a time, until you are a master of very thin crespelle. Do not add more than 2 cups total, including the original water and club soda.

To cook the crespelle: Heat a medium nonstick skillet over medium heat, and brush it with melted butter. When the skillet is hot and the butter is sizzling, with the skillet in one hand, pour in a scant ¼ cup batter and immediately rotate the skillet to coat the bottom of the pan evenly and quickly with the batter. Set the pan back on the heat, and cook until the crêpe is golden on the underside and the edges begin to curl from the sides of the pan, about 1 minute or so. Flip, and cook the other side, 30 seconds to a minute more. Remove to a plate.

Continue with the remaining batter, brushing the skillet with melted butter each time, and stacking the crespelle on the plate.

Crespelle with Herb Pesto

Crespelle con Pesto di Erbe

Serves 4

FOR THE HERB PESTO

1½ cups loosely packed
fresh basil leaves

1½ cups loosely packed fresh
Italian parsley leaves

2 garlic cloves, crushed and peeled

¼ cup pine nuts, toasted

2 teaspoons fresh thyme leaves

Kosher salt

⅓ cup extra-virgin olive oil

¼ cup freshly grated Grana Padano

FOR ASSEMBLING THE CRESPELLE

Unsalted butter, for the baking dish

2 cups (1 pound) good-
quality fresh ricotta

1½ cups half-and-half

1 cup freshly grated Grana Padano

Kosher salt and freshly
ground black pepper

8 Crespelle (preceding recipe)

This recipe includes one of my go-to herb combinations, but use your family's favorites or whatever herbs you have on hand in your garden or refrigerator. It works best with any stems removed, and with softer herbs. I usually pick whatever is growing abundantly in my herb garden. If you do not have these in your garden, leafy greens like spinach or Swiss chard, mixed with parsley or basil, would also make a good pesto for this dish. The pine nuts can be replaced with walnuts, almonds, or hazelnuts— whatever you have in the house. Keep in mind, if you use strong herbs like sage or thyme, that you should spread just a thin layer on the crêpes, and add a bit more ricotta. If, on the other hand, you made a pesto of milder vegetable leaves, be more generous with the pesto.

For the pesto: Combine the basil, parsley, garlic, pine nuts, thyme, and 1 teaspoon salt in a mini–food processor. Pulse to make a coarse paste. With the processor running, add the olive oil in a slow stream, to make a smooth pesto. Transfer to a small bowl, and stir in the grated cheese. Remove and reserve 2 tablespoons.

To assemble: Preheat the oven to 400 degrees. Butter a 9-by-13-inch baking dish. In a large bowl, combine the ricotta, ½ cup half-and-half, ½ cup grated cheese, ½ teaspoon salt, and several grinds of pepper. Stir until smooth. In a spouted measuring cup, whisk together the remaining cup of half-and-half and the reserved 2 tablespoons pesto.

Lay the crespelle out on your work surface. Spread them with pesto almost to the edges. Dollop the ricotta mixture on top, and spread that almost to the edges. Fold the crespelle in half, then in half again to make rounded triangles.

Pour about a quarter of the half-and-half mixture into the bottom of the prepared baking dish, and lay in the crespelle, slightly overlapping them. Pour the remaining half-and-half mixture over the top. Sprinkle with the remaining ½ cup grated cheese. Bake until the crespelle are bubbly with crisp edges, 25 to 30 minutes.

Crespelle Manicotti with Spinach

Manicotti di Crespelle con Spinaci

Serves 6

Unsalted butter, at room temperature, for the baking dish

3 tablespoons extra-virgin olive oil

4 garlic cloves, crushed and peeled

2 bunches mature spinach (not baby) (about 1¼ pounds), stemmed

Kosher salt

Peperoncino flakes

3 cups (1½ pounds) good-quality fresh ricotta

1 large egg, beaten

8 ounces young provola, grated

2 cups freshly grated Grana Padano

12 Crespelle (page 86)

5 cups Marinara (page 7)

Manicotti are a much-loved baked pasta in our family, but in this case I use crespelle instead of fresh pasta to envelop the ricotta stuffing. If you have crespelle in the freezer, as I usually do, it is a faster preparation; just be careful not to overstuff the crespelle, because they puff up in the baking process. For years, I've asked myself where the name "manicotti" comes from. Then, one day, I figured it out. When I was in a refugee camp in Trieste, I was enrolled in a Catholic school, and to supplement my tuition I would help the nuns in the kitchen. They wore big aprons, and on their arms, to protect the sleeves of their habits, they had tubes made out of white cloth with elastic edges on both sides. These sleeves covered their arms from wrist to elbow, and they were called "manicotti"; hence the name of tubular stuffed pasta that we now know as manicotti.

Preheat the oven to 400 degrees. Butter a 9-by-13-inch baking dish.

Heat a large skillet over medium-high heat, and add the olive oil. When the oil is hot, add the garlic, and cook until it's sizzling, about 1 minute. Add the spinach, and season with 1 teaspoon salt and a pinch of peperoncino. Cook, tossing occasionally, until the spinach is wilted, 4 to 5 minutes.

Put the spinach into a colander to drain. Discard the garlic. Press on the spinach to remove any excess water. Chop it, and place it in a large bowl. Add the ricotta, egg, provola, 1 cup Grana Padano, and 1 teaspoon salt. Mix well to combine.

Lay the crespelle out on your work surface, and divide the filling among them, spreading it on the bottom halves. Fold the sides in and then roll them up, like little burritos.

Spread about 1½ cups of the marinara sauce in the bottom of the prepared baking dish, and arrange the crespelle, seam side down, in one layer. Pour 1½ cups sauce over the top. Sprinkle with the remaining 1 cup grated Grana Padano. Bake until the cheese is golden brown and crusty and the sauce is bubbly, 40 to 45 minutes. Warm the remaining 2 cups of marinara to serve at the table.

Mushroom Ragù with Greens over Polenta

Polenta con Ragù di Funghi e Verdure

Serves 6 to 8

FOR THE MUSHROOM RAGÙ

¼ cup extra-virgin olive oil

3 leeks, white and light-green parts, halved vertically, sliced

2 pounds mixed mushrooms (such as button, cremini, oyster, shiitake, chanterelle), thickly sliced

Kosher salt

2 teaspoons chopped fresh rosemary leaves

2 fresh bay leaves

1 cup low-sodium chicken or vegetable stock

FOR THE POLENTA

1 tablespoon extra-virgin olive oil

1 fresh bay leaf

Kosher salt

1½ cups coarse yellow polenta

4 tablespoons unsalted butter, cut into pieces

½ cup freshly grated Grana Padano, plus more for serving

Many of you write to me about my vegetable recipes. Italian cuisine is a lot about cooking with vegetables, not only as a side dish but also, as in this case, as a main course. Yes, you could add bacon or sausages, but I love cooking and eating vegetables on their own, especially when they are paired with a starch like polenta, or rice or pasta. I suggest you make the mushroom ragù first, then the polenta, so it is piping hot when you serve it.

I love polenta and its versatility. Coming from the north, we ate a lot of it. Polenta for breakfast with warm milk and honey, fried and pan-seared polenta served with melted cheese as a sandwich for lunch, and, for dinner, polenta with sautéed vegetables or braised meat, or, of course, with game meats in the winter.

For the mushroom ragù: Heat the olive oil in a large Dutch oven over medium heat. When the oil is hot, add the leeks and mushrooms. Season with 2 teaspoons salt and the rosemary. Stir to combine. Cook, stirring occasionally, until the mushrooms are lightly browned and wilted, 8 to 10 minutes. Add the bay leaves and stock. Cover, and cook until the mushrooms are very tender, about 15 minutes more. Remove the bay leaves.

For the polenta: Combine 6 cups water, the olive oil, bay leaf, and 2 teaspoons salt in a large saucepan, and bring the water to a simmer over medium-low heat.

Whisking slowly, stream the polenta into the pot through the fingers of one hand. Whisk constantly at this point, to avoid lumps. Once all of the polenta is added, adjust the heat so a few small bubbles pop to the surface. Continue to cook and stir, making sure you get the corners and bottom of the pan, until the polenta is thick and pulls away from the sides of the pan, 30 to 35 minutes.

Discard the bay leaf, and beat in the butter and cheese.

For the greens: Heat the olive oil in a large skillet over medium-high heat. When the oil is hot, add the garlic, and cook until it's sizzling, about

¼ cup extra-virgin olive oil

5 sliced garlic cloves

2 bunches escarole
(about 1½ pounds), leaves
separated and trimmed

Kosher salt

½ teaspoon peperoncino flakes

30 seconds. Add the escarole, and season with 2 teaspoons salt and the peperoncino. Toss well. Cover, and cook until the escarole has wilted, about 10 minutes. Uncover, and increase the heat to reduce away any liquid in the pan, about 1 minute. Remove and discard the garlic.

To serve: Spoon a mound of polenta on a plate, top with the braised escarole, and then spoon the mushroom ragù over it all. Some grated Grana Padano cheese is a great finale.

Risotto with Asparagus and Favas

Risotto con Asparagi e Fave

Serves 6

Kosher salt

2 pounds fresh fava beans
in the pod, shelled

6 to 7 cups low-sodium chicken
or vegetable stock or water

3 tablespoons extra-virgin olive oil

4 scallions, chopped, white
and green parts separated

2 medium shallots, chopped

2 cups Arborio or Carnaroli rice

1 cup dry white wine

1 bunch medium-thick asparagus,
tough ends removed, lower
half peeled, stalks cut into
1-inch segments (keep the tips
separate from the rest)

2 tablespoons unsalted
butter, cut into pieces

½ cup freshly grated Grana Padano

Making a risotto is all about the technique, but, for me, the flavoring is all about capturing the tastes and aromas of the seasons. Here we are in spring. My family knows I love to make risotto. Risotto with fish, with meat, with vegetables, and even the classic risotto alla milanese with saffron are all in my wheelhouse. Not to toot my own horn, but my family tells me I make the best risotto and it is my *piatto forte*.

Bring a large pot of salted water to a boil. Set a large bowl of water with ice next to the pot. Add the shelled favas to the boiling water. Bring it back to a boil, and cook for 1 minute. Remove the favas to the ice bath. Drain, pat them dry, and peel the tough outer skins from the favas. You should have about 1 heaping cup peeled favas.

Discard the cooking water, and add the stock or water to the pot. Warm over low heat.

Heat the olive oil in a large, shallow Dutch oven over medium heat. Add the scallion whites and shallots, and cook, stirring often, until they're wilted, about 2 minutes. Add the rice, and stir to coat in the oil. Cook and stir until the edges of the grains are translucent, about 2 minutes. Pour in the white wine. Adjust the heat so everything is simmering, and cook, stirring often, until the wine is almost absorbed. Add enough stock to cover, and simmer until it's almost absorbed. Add the asparagus (but not the tips) after the first addition of stock has been absorbed. Continue stirring and adding more stock as it gets absorbed.

Once you've added about two-thirds of the stock, add the favas, asparagus tips, and scallion greens. Cook and stir, adding the remaining stock, until the rice is creamy and a bit loose but still al dente, about 18 minutes total from the first addition of stock.

Remove the rice from the heat. Add the butter pieces, and mix vigorously to incorporate them. Stir in the grated cheese, and serve.

Pumpkin Risotto

Risotto di Zucca

Serves 6

6 to 7 cups low-sodium chicken or vegetable stock or water

3 tablespoons extra-virgin olive oil

1 medium onion, finely chopped

3 cups small (½-inch) cubes of peeled pumpkin or other winter squash

8 fresh sage leaves, chopped

2 cups Arborio or Carnaroli rice

Kosher salt

½ cup dry white wine

¼ teaspoon freshly grated nutmeg

2 tablespoons unsalted butter, cut into pieces

½ cup freshly grated Grana Padano

2-ounce piece Gorgonzola Dolce

Pumpkin is a favorite in the region of Emilia-Romagna, where they often use it in the stuffing for fresh pasta. I first saw pumpkin risotto there while traveling on a family vacation. I used to take my two children with me on every vacation—even work vacations that were about tasting food, seeing Italian wine producers, and learning about Italian products. Sometimes they were bored, especially if some of the meals became marathons, but other times they were able to experience games of hide in seek in fairy-tale-like wine cellars, or visit a dairy farm with all the animals to see how Grana Padano was made. Here is a recipe for the fall or winter vegetable season. The grated Grana Padano is a given, but to counteract the sweetness of winter squash I crumble some Gorgonzola Dolce on top. It makes a wonderful finish for this risotto, but if you're not a fan, you can also finish with a drizzle of balsamic reduction (page 68).

Put the stock in a saucepan, and warm it over low heat.

Heat the olive oil in a large, shallow Dutch oven over medium heat. Add the onion and pumpkin, and cook, stirring often, until the onion is wilted, about 5 minutes. Add the sage, and let it sizzle for a minute. Add the rice, and stir to coat it in the oil. Cook and stir until the edges of the grains are translucent, about 2 minutes. Season with 2 teaspoons salt. Pour in the white wine, and add the nutmeg. Adjust the heat so everything is simmering, and cook, stirring often, until the wine is almost absorbed.

Add enough stock to cover, and simmer until it's almost absorbed. Continue stirring and adding more stock as it gets absorbed until the rice is creamy and a bit loose but still al dente, about 18 minutes total from the first addition of stock.

Remove the rice from the heat. Add the butter pieces, and mix vigorously to incorporate them. Stir in the grated Grana Padano. Serve immediately in shallow bowls, and crumble the Gorgonzola over the top.

Shrimp and Tomato Risotto

Risotto di Gamberi e Pomodoro

Serves 6

5 tablespoons extra-virgin olive oil

1 medium onion, finely chopped

2 cups Arborio or Carnaroli rice

Kosher salt

¾ cup dry white wine

2 cups halved ripe cherry tomatoes

2 garlic cloves, sliced

¼ teaspoon peperoncino flakes

1 pound medium shrimp, peeled, deveined, tails on

½ cup loosely packed fresh basil leaves, shredded

2 tablespoons unsalted butter, cut into pieces

½ cup freshly grated Grana Padano

This risotto sings of summer, but it could be made any time of the year. The one thing to be watchful of here is not to overcook the shrimp. You can turn this risotto into a scallop risotto or a chicken risotto by substituting the protein of your choice; again, just be mindful of the cooking time for each. I use plain water here as the cooking liquid so it doesn't take away from the delicate flavor of the shrimp and the ripe summer vegetables can also shine through. The myth that you must have a boiling pot of good stock does not always hold true.

Put 6 to 7 cups water in a saucepan, and warm over low heat.

Heat 3 tablespoons of the olive oil in a large shallow Dutch oven over medium heat. Add the onion, and cook, stirring often, until it's wilted, about 5 minutes. Add the rice, and stir to coat it in the oil. Cook and stir until the edges are translucent, about 2 minutes. Season with 2 teaspoons salt. Pour in the white wine. Adjust the heat so everything is simmering, and cook, stirring often, until the wine is almost absorbed. Add enough water to cover, and simmer until it's almost absorbed. Continue stirring and adding more water as it gets absorbed until the rice is creamy and a bit loose but still al dente, about 18 minutes total from the first addition of water.

Meanwhile, heat a large skillet over medium-high heat. Add the remaining 2 tablespoons olive oil. When the oil is hot, add the cherry tomatoes and garlic and season with the peperoncino and 1 teaspoon salt. Toss to coat everything in the oil, and cook until the tomatoes begin to give up their juices, about 2 minutes. Add the shrimp and cook, tossing occasionally, until they're just cooked through and the tomatoes are juicy, about 2 minutes. Stir in the basil. Stir this mixture into the rice as it is finishing cooking, and simmer for a minute or two to blend the flavors.

Remove the risotto from the heat. Add the butter pieces, and mix vigorously to incorporate them. Stir in the grated cheese, and serve.

Barley Risotto with Cabbage and Sausage

Risotto di Farro con Verza e Salsiccia

Serves 6 to 8

Kosher salt

2 fresh bay leaves

1½ cups pearl barley

3 tablespoons extra-virgin olive oil

3 links sweet Italian sausage (about 10 ounces), removed from casings

1 medium onion, chopped

2 teaspoons chopped fresh thyme

½ medium head savoy cabbage, cored, coarsely chopped

½ teaspoon peperoncino flakes

1 cup dry white wine

6 to 7 cups low-sodium chicken or vegetable stock or water

3 tablespoons unsalted butter, cut into pieces

¼ cup chopped fresh Italian parsley

½ cup freshly grated Grana Padano

Tanya absolutely loves the combination of cabbage and sausage, and this dish is one of her favorites. Today we are all cooking with more and different grains. Barley is an ancient grain, one of the first grains cultivated, more than eight thousand years ago, and is used around the world. Every region of Italy uses it—as flour to make pasta, for breads and porridges, in soups, as a *contorno,* in stews—and I use it here in a risotto. Barley does not release starch as short-grain rice does, and so, when making a barley risotto, I cook the barley separately, drain it, and add it to the flavoring of the risotto I want to make—in this case, cabbage and sausage. Then I apply the last step of a regular risotto, *mantecare,* mixing the flavored barley with butter and grated Grana Padano to make it creamy. I par-cook the barley like pasta in this recipe, since it takes much longer to cook than rice.

Bring a large saucepan with 4 quarts of salted water to a boil with the bay leaves. Add the barley, and simmer until about halfway cooked (tender on the outside but still with a bite in the center), 25 to 30 minutes. Drain well.

Heat a large Dutch oven over medium heat. Add the olive oil, and crumble in the sausage. Cook, breaking up the sausage with a wooden spoon, until it's browned, 3 to 4 minutes. Add the onion and thyme, and cook, stirring occasionally, until the onion begins to wilt, about 4 minutes. Add the cabbage and season with 1½ teaspoons salt and the peperoncino. Cover, and cook, stirring occasionally, until the cabbage wilts, about 5 minutes.

Add the drained barley, and cook and stir, uncovered, about 2 minutes. Add the wine, bring to a simmer, and cook until it's absorbed. Add stock to cover. Simmer, stirring occasionally, until the liquid is almost absorbed. Continue adding stock as needed until the barley is cooked and the cabbage is tender, 15 to 20 minutes more.

Remove the barley from the heat. Add the butter pieces and parsley, and mix vigorously to incorporate them. Stir in the grated cheese, and serve.

Fresh Pasta for Pappardelle/Tagliatelle/ Quadrucci/Fuzi/Pasutice/Anolini

Pasta Fresca per Pappardelle/Tagliatelle/Quadrucci/Fuzi/Pasutice/Anolini

Makes 1 pound pasta dough

2 cups all-purpose flour, plus more as needed

2 large eggs

3 tablespoons extra-virgin olive oil

¼ cup ice water, plus more as needed

This is the dough I make at home. Simple to prepare and easy to roll out, it keeps well for 2 days tightly wrapped in the refrigerator and 2 months in the freezer. I make all different shapes of pasta with this dough; fettuccine, tagliatelle, quadrucci for soup, and pappardelle, garganelli (fuzi), maltagliati (pasutice). Often, in my nonna Rosa's kitchen, all the leftover pasta dough was rolled out and cut into varying shapes to be used for soup; we had a potpourri of pasta shapes, and not one little corner of the dough went to waste. Here are instructions on how to cut some of the shapes that are used in some of the recipes in this book, plus a filled pasta you can serve in chicken broth or the Mixed Meat Broth on page 50.

Making fresh pasta is a beautiful way to connect with the family, especially children when they are small and are happy to get their hands in the dough. I recall that my mother, Erminia, would always ask Joe and Tanya to help her when they were little, and she would tell them stories of her childhood as they kneaded the dough. These stories remained with them, and they passed on their love of pasta making to all five of my grandchildren. Now these children are away at college, and Nonna Mima, as they endearingly called her, is no longer with us, but I get Zoom calls for quick recipes they can make at school, and orders for what they want to eat when they come home from college. Pasta fresca is always on the list.

Put the flour in a food processor, and pulse to aerate. Combine the eggs, olive oil, and ice water in a spouted measuring cup, and beat with a fork to combine.

With the processor running, add the egg mixture through the feed tube until a dough begins to form around the blade. Process until the dough is soft and springy and forms a loose ball around the blade. (If the dough is too loose to form a ball, add a tablespoon or two more flour; if it is too crumbly, add a little more water.) Turn the dough onto a floured countertop, and knead a few times to bring it together into a ball. →

← Wrap in plastic wrap and let it rest for 30 minutes at room temperature. Cut the rested dough into four pieces. Roll one piece through a pasta machine on the widest setting to stretch it, fold like a letter, and feed the side of the folded dough where the two ends meet through the machine again. Repeat once more, same as before, to smooth out the dough and create an even rectangle. Repeat with the remaining pieces of dough. Switch to the next-lower setting, and roll each piece through only once. Continue to take the machine down a setting (or two, if the dough rolls through too easily; it depends on your machine) and roll the pieces through until you have four thin pieces about the width of your pasta machine. Cut each piece in half crosswise to get eight pieces.

PASTA SHAPES

FOR PAPPARDELLE: Roll the floured pieces up lengthwise, like a cigar, and cut them into 1-inch ribbons. Gently twirl them, and form into loose nests on a floured baking sheet.

FOR TAGLIATELLE: Roll as for pappardelle, but cut into ½-inch ribbons.

FOR QUADRUCCI: Make tagliatelle, and then cut crosswise into little squares; use in soups.

FOR PASUTICE: Cut the eight pieces lengthwise into three strips each. Cut across the ribbons on the diagonal at 2-inch intervals to make diamonds. Toss the pasutice with abundant flour, and lay them in a single layer on a floured baking sheet. Cover with a dishcloth, flour the cloth, and layer more pasutice as needed.

FOR FUZI: Make the pasutice diamonds. Starting at one corner of each diamond, roll the piece of dough diagonally around a floured chopstick (or something similar, like a thin-handled wooden spoon the thickness of a large straw) and overlap the ends to make a tube. Press on the overlapping ends to seal, and slide the dough off the chopstick. Spread on a floured baking sheet. (Use two baking sheets, if needed; don't stack these or you'll crush them.)

FOR ANOLINI: Mix 1½ cups fresh ricotta, 1 egg yolk, ⅓ cup freshly grated Grana Padano, 2 tablespoons chopped parsley, and a pinch of salt in a bowl. Roll the pasta into sheets, as described opposite, but don't cut the sheets in half. Use a 1-inch round cutter to mark as many rounds as possible in half of the sheets, not cutting all the way through the dough. Dollop about ½ teaspoon ricotta filling in each of the circles, and wet the edges with your finger dipped in water. Lay the remaining sheets over the top to cover the filling, gently draping and stretching to cover all of the mounds of filling. Use the cutter to cut through both pieces of dough for all of the mounds. Pull away any excess pasta to separate the individual anolini. Press the edges of the circles together to seal, and dust them with flour. Place them on floured baking sheets.

Fuzi with Chicken Ragù

Fuzi con Sugo di Pollo

Serves 6

1 quart low-sodium chicken stock

½ cup dried porcini

6 bone-in, skinless chicken thighs (about 2¼ pounds)

Kosher salt and freshly ground black pepper

3 tablespoons extra-virgin olive oil, plus more for drizzling

1 medium onion, finely chopped

3 tablespoons tomato paste

4 ounces chicken livers, trimmed, finely chopped

2 fresh bay leaves

1 sprig fresh rosemary

¼ teaspoon ground cloves

1 cup dry white wine

12 ounces mixed mushrooms (such as button, cremini, oyster, shiitake, chanterelle), sliced

¼ cup chopped fresh Italian parsley

1 pound fresh fuzi (preceding recipe)

½ cup freshly grated Grana Padano

This was a traditional Sunday dish for my family when I was growing up. On Saturdays, Nonna Rosa would prepare one or two of the chickens that roamed our courtyard, butchering them, plucking the feathers, and cutting them into pieces. On Sunday morning, she would make soup from the neck, head, innards, and feet; from the rest, she made sugo or ragù sauce. Courtyard chickens always took a little longer to cook, and while the sugo was cooking we would make fuzi. With a few slices of prosciutto and a salad as an appetizer, that was our Sunday dinner. Fuzi are a rendition of garganelli, but when you are making them fresh each piece of diamond-shaped dough has to be gently wrapped around a finger or wooden dowel and two opposite corners of the diamond pressed together. The fuzi are pulled off the finger and, like soldiers, placed next to each other on a wooden board, to dry and wait to be dumped into a pot of boiling salted water, drained, and tossed with the chicken ragù topped with grated cheese.

Warm the stock in a small saucepan over low heat. Ladle 1 cup stock over the porcini in a spouted measuring cup, and let the mushrooms soften, about 10 minutes. Drain and chop the porcini, reserving the soaking liquid.

Season the chicken with 1 teaspoon salt and several grinds of pepper. Heat the olive oil in a large Dutch oven over medium heat. Add the chicken pieces, in batches if needed, and brown on both sides, about 2 minutes per side. Remove to a plate as they brown.

Once all of the chicken is out of the pot, add the onion, and cook until it begins to soften, about 4 minutes. Make a space in the pan, and add the tomato paste to that spot. Cook and stir the tomato paste there for a minute, until it turns a shade or so darker, then stir into the onion pieces. Add the chicken livers. Cook and stir until they're no longer raw on the outside, about 2 minutes. Add the chopped porcini, the bay leaves, rosemary, and cloves. Pour in the white wine, and simmer until it's reduced by half, about 2 minutes.

Add the chicken pieces, and pour in the porcini-soaking liquid, leaving any grit that remains in the bottom of the cup. Ladle in enough stock just to cover the chicken. Adjust the heat so the sauce is simmering gently. Cook, covered, for 20 minutes.

Uncover, and add the fresh mushrooms and the remaining stock. Stir, and continue to simmer until the chicken is falling from the bone and the sauce is thick, about 20 to 25 minutes more.

Turn off the heat, and remove the chicken pieces. Discard the bones and shred the chicken back into the pot. Discard the rosemary stem and bay leaves. Taste, and season with salt if needed.

To serve: Bring a large pot of salted water to a boil for the pasta. Bring the sauce to a simmer, and stir in the parsley. Add the fuzi to the boiling water, and cook until al dente, 3 to 4 minutes. In the meantime, remove half of the sauce to a large skillet, and bring it to a simmer. Remove the fuzi with a spider strainer directly into the simmering sauce. Drizzle with a little olive oil, and toss to coat the pasta in the sauce, adding more sauce and a little pasta water if it seems dry. Remove from the heat, stir in the grated cheese, and serve, with the extra sauce on the side.

Istrian Pasutice with Mixed Seafood

Pasutice all'Istriana con Pesce

Serves 6

Kosher salt

⅓ cup extra-virgin olive oil, plus more for drizzling

6 garlic cloves, thinly sliced

8 ounces medium shrimp, peeled, deveined, tails removed

8 ounces sea scallops, side muscles ("feet") removed, halved if large

One 24-ounce jar tomato passata

¼ teaspoon peperoncino flakes

2 pounds mussels, scrubbed

1 pound pasutice (page 97)

¼ cup chopped fresh Italian parsley

Living near the sea as a small child, I would spend days at the beach, picking critters off the rocky coastline. My bounty might include small crabs, little snails, mussels, barnacles, and clams. In the evening, my hard work was rewarded with a plate of fresh homemade pasta and mixed seafood sauce. This is one of my favorite dishes. It is quick: once you have the pasutice made, the sauce takes 15 minutes. Pasutice are rolled pasta dough cut into 1-inch diamond shapes. Since the pasutice are flat, they have a tendency to stick to each other once in the water. Make sure you have plenty of salted water boiling, and drop the pasutice in one handful at a time in a sawing motion to separate them from one another when they hit the water, while stirring the water with a wooden spoon with your other hand. Keep on mixing until the water returns to a boil.

Bring a large pot of salted water to a boil for the pasta.

Heat a large Dutch oven over medium-high heat. Add the olive oil. When the oil is hot, scatter in the garlic, and cook until it's sizzling, about 30 seconds. Add the shrimp and scallops, and season with 1 teaspoon salt. Cook and toss until the seafood is just translucent, about 2 minutes. Remove to a plate.

Add the passata, 1 cup water, and the peperoncino. Bring the liquid to a simmer, and cook until it's slightly thickened, 5 to 7 minutes. Add the mussels, toss, and bring the liquid back to a simmer. Cover, and cook until the mussels begin to open, 3 to 4 minutes. Add the shrimp and scallops, and return to a simmer. Simmer just until all of the seafood is cooked through, 2 to 3 minutes more. Discard any mussels that don't open.

Meanwhile, add the pasta to the boiling water (see headnote for detailed procedure) and cook until al dente, 3 to 4 minutes. Remove the pasta with a spider strainer to the simmering sauce. Add the parsley and a drizzle of olive oil, and toss to coat the pasta in the sauce, adding a little more pasta water if it seems dry.

Pappardelle with Lamb Ragù

Pappardelle al Ragù d'Agnello

Serves 4 to 6

2 cups low-sodium chicken stock

½ cup dried porcini

1 small onion, coarsely chopped

1 small carrot, coarsely chopped

1 stalk celery, coarsely chopped

3 tablespoons extra-virgin olive oil

1 pound ground lamb

1 red bell pepper, seeded, finely chopped

Kosher salt

Peperoncino flakes

2 teaspoons chopped fresh rosemary

½ cup dry red wine

One 28-ounce can whole San Marzano tomatoes, crushed by hand

1 pound fresh pappardelle (page 97)

¼ cup chopped fresh Italian parsley

½ cup freshly grated Grana Padano

Bologna, capital of the Emilia-Romagna region in Italy, is nicknamed La Grassa, or "The Fat." This has a political meaning, but it's also a reference to the amazing food from the region. Emilia-Romagna is the home of fresh pasta and stuffed pastas. There they have many dishes of baked pastas rich with cheese and cream, and this is where Bolognese sauce comes from. Everybody loves a Bolognese sauce, and this recipe is similar, with a slightly different flavor. Here I make it with lamb instead of beef and add lots of vegetables—onion, carrot, celery, and red bell pepper. The vegetables bring a freshness and sweetness to the lamb. Paired with the homemade pappardelle, they make a delicious dish. The sauce here is double what you will need for one recipe of pappardelle, but it freezes very well, and will also work well with dried pasta, like spaghetti or rigatoni.

Warm the chicken stock in a small saucepan over low heat. Add the porcini, and let them soak until softened, about 10 minutes. Remove and chop them, reserving the stock.

Put the onion, carrot, and celery in a food processor, and pulse to make a smooth paste or pestata. Heat a medium Dutch oven over medium heat. Add the olive oil. When the oil is hot, crumble in the ground lamb, and add the bell pepper. Cook and stir until the lamb is finely crumbled and no longer pink, about 4 minutes. Add the pestata, and stir to combine. Cook and stir until the pestata dries out, about 2 to 3 minutes. Season with 2 teaspoons salt and a pinch of peperoncino, and stir in the rosemary and chopped porcini.

Add the red wine, and simmer to reduce the liquid by half. Add the tomatoes, 1 cup water sloshed in the tomato can, the stock in which the porcini soaked (leaving any grit left in the bottom of the pot), and bay leaves. Adjust the heat so the sauce is simmering, and cook until it is very thick and flavorful, 45 to 50 minutes. Discard the bay leaves. Remove half of the sauce to a container, and let it cool before refrigerating or freezing. (Or save a little to serve at the table.)

When you're ready to serve, bring a large pot of salted water to a boil for the pasta. Add the pappardelle. Once the water is again boiling, cook until al dente, 4 to 5 minutes. Fish out the pappardelle with tongs or a spider strainer, and add the pasta to the simmering sauce. Add the parsley, and toss to coat the pasta with the sauce, adding a little pasta water if it seems dry. Remove from the heat, sprinkle with the grated cheese, toss, and serve. Serve some of the extra sauce on the side, if desired.

Ricotta Cavatelli with Arugula

Cavatelli di Ricotta con la Rucola

Serves 6

FOR THE CAVATELLI

2 cups all-purpose flour, plus more for dusting

1¾ cups good-quality fresh ricotta

1 large egg

Kosher salt

FOR THE SAUCE

¼ cup extra-virgin olive oil

4 garlic cloves, sliced

2 teaspoons fresh rosemary leaves, chopped

One 28-ounce can whole San Marzano tomatoes, crushed by hand

Kosher salt

½ teaspoon peperoncino flakes

2 bunches arugula, cleaned, tough stems removed

½ cup freshly grated pecorino

1 small piece ricotta salata, for grating

The older women in Puglia and Calabria make cavatelli with lightning speed. It is inspiring to watch the dough rolling off their fingers and flicked onto a board. They do it from muscle memory while they chat away about local events. To lighten the cavatelli, traditionally made of semolina flour, they add ricotta—usually ricotta they made themselves—to the flour. So that's what I call for you to do here. They also add any bitter greens they have around or have foraged. If you can't find bunches of mature arugula (or think it's too bitter), you can use spinach instead, or a combination of the two.

For the cavatelli: Put the flour in a food processor and pulse to aerate it. Mix the ricotta, egg, and ½ teaspoon salt in a bowl, and add this to the food processor. Process until the dough forms a loose ball on the blade, about 1 minute, adding a little more flour or a little water if needed. Place the dough on a floured counter, and knead a few times to bring it together. Wrap it in plastic wrap, and let it rest for 30 minutes.

Cut the rested dough into quarters, and keep the pieces covered if you're not working with them. Dust two rimmed baking sheets with flour. Dust your work surface with flour (and continue to dust if the dough sticks later on). Pinch off a ball of dough from one of the quarters, and roll it to the thickness of a pencil. Cut into ½-inch segments, and roll those into rough ovals in the palms of your floured hands. Press one or two fingers into the middle of the oval and roll back and forth to make a concavity in the dough, flicking it off your finger on the way up. Repeat with the remaining dough, resting the cavatelli on the floured baking sheets.

Bring a large pot of salted water to a boil.

To make the sauce: Heat a large skillet over medium heat. Add the olive oil. When the oil is hot, add the garlic and rosemary, and cook until they're sizzling, about 1 minute. Stir in the tomatoes, rinse out the can with 1 cup pasta water, and add that as well. Add 2 teaspoons salt and the peperoncino. Bring to a simmer, and cook until it's thickened, 10 to 15 minutes.

When the sauce is almost ready, shake the cavatelli into a colander to get rid of any excess flour, and add them to the boiling water. Bring the water back to a simmer. Cook the cavatelli till they're al dente—about 5 to 6 minutes after they float to the surface—adding the arugula in the last minute or two. (Taste one cavatello before adding the arugula to be sure.) Scoop the cavatelli and arugula out with a spider strainer, and add them to the simmering sauce. Toss to coat the cavatelli in the sauce, adding a little pasta water if the sauce seems dry. Off heat, sprinkle with the grated pecorino and toss. Serve, grating the ricotta salata over the top of each portion.

Gnocchi with Sauce from Erice

Gnocchi con Salsa di Erice

Serves 6

FOR THE GNOCCHI

3 large russet potatoes, peel left on

1 teaspoon kosher salt

1 large egg, beaten

2 cups all-purpose flour,
plus more as needed

FOR THE SAUCE

2 cups fresh basil leaves

½ cup slivered almonds, toasted

2 garlic cloves, crushed and peeled

Kosher salt

¼ cup extra-virgin olive oil

2 large eggs, hard-boiled,
finely chopped

½ cup grated pecorino

When they were little, I'd always have my kids and grandkids help me with making gnocchi (I did the same thing as a small child). They loved rolling out the dough—it's like playing with Play-Doh—and their small fingers are perfect for rolling the gnocchi off the fork to give them the perfect shape for sauce to adhere to. Gnocchi are much simpler to make than most people think; once you have the knack, you will be making them often. So read my instructions well! The two crucial steps are: first, after ricing the potatoes, spread them out and let them cool completely, and, second, do not overwork the dough. This dough is different from regular pasta dough, which you have to knead to develop the gluten. In making gnocchi, all you need is to mix the potatoes, eggs, and flour until everything is amalgamated. Too much kneading will require more flour and will make the gnocchi stodgy and heavy. In shaping them, you will need more flour so they do not stick; keep on sprinkling flour on the work surface and on your hands, shaping the gnocchi quickly without overworking them.

For the gnocchi: Put the potatoes in a pot with water to cover. Bring to a simmer, and cook until tender all the way through when pierced with a knife, about 20 to 25 minutes. Drain, and let cool just until you can handle them; then peel them and press them through a potato ricer into an even layer on your countertop. Sprinkle the salt over them evenly. Let them cool.

When the potatoes have cooled, form them into a mound with a small well in the center. Add the egg. Work the egg into the potatoes with a fork; then gradually work in the 2 cups flour, switching to your hands when the dough becomes workable. Continue to knead the dough, dusting with flour as needed, until the dough comes together in a cohesive mass. (If you cut through the dough, the interior will look like a cross section of cookie dough.)

Dust your work surface and two baking sheets with flour. Divide the dough into six pieces, keeping all the pieces you're not working on covered with a cloth as you go. Roll one piece of dough into a ½-inch rope on the floured counter, and cut into ½-inch pieces. Roll the pieces into rough balls, then roll them down along the curved tines of a fork with your thumb to create ridges on one side and a concave depression on the other side. Repeat with the remaining dough.

Bring a large pot of salted water to a boil.

To make the salsa di Erice: Combine the basil, almonds, garlic, and 1 teaspoon salt in a mini–food processor, and pulse to make a paste. With the processor running, add the olive oil in a slow stream to make a smooth pesto. Transfer to a serving bowl, and fold in the chopped egg.

Shake the excess flour from the gnocchi, and add them to the boiling water. Cook until they're tender—2 to 4 minutes after they begin to float, depending on how large you've made them. Remove them with a spider strainer to a serving bowl. Ladle in about ½ cup pasta-cooking water. Sprinkle with the pecorino, toss well to coat, and serve, adding a little more pasta water if the sauce still seems dry.

Sweet Potato Chickpea Gnocchi with Gorgonzola

Gnocchi di Patate Dolci e Ceci al Gorgonzola

Serves 6 to 8

2 medium sweet potatoes, peel left on (about 10 ounces each)

Kosher salt

1 cup good-quality fresh ricotta

1 large egg, beaten

¼ teaspoon freshly grated nutmeg

1½ cups chickpea flour

1½ to 2 cups all-purpose flour, plus more for working the dough and dusting

4 tablespoons unsalted butter

1½ cups heavy cream

6 ounces Gorgonzola Dolce, crumbled

½ cup freshly grated Grana Padano

As my grandkids grew, some of them asked for gluten-free options, and this is a gnocchi recipe I made for them with sweet potatoes and gluten-free chickpea flour. The Gorgonzola makes a quick and luscious sauce, but you could also dress this with the rabbit from page 153. Just remove the meat from the bones and shred it. The chickpea flour adds nuttiness, but you can make the recipe with all regular flour or entirely with gluten-free flour. This is a very rich dish, so a small portion goes a long way.

Put the unpeeled sweet potatoes in a pot with salted water to cover. Boil until tender, about 20 minutes (don't overcook, or they'll take in too much water and the gnocchi will be dense). Drain well. While they're still hot, peel them and press them through a ricer onto the counter in a single layer. Season with 1 teaspoon salt, and let them cool completely.

When the potatoes are cooled, gather them into a mound and make an indentation in the center. Add the ricotta, egg, and nutmeg, and begin mixing with a fork, pulling the sweet potato into the egg little by little. Add the chickpea flour and 1½ cups of the all-purpose flour. Mix with the fork to form a dough; then begin to knead it with floured hands and a bench scraper to bring the dough together. If it is still very wet, add more flour, a few tablespoons at a time, until the dough forms a slightly sticky but cohesive ball.

Dust two rimmed baking sheets with flour, and divide the dough into six portions, keeping all the pieces you're not working on covered with a kitchen towel as you go. Roll one piece into a ¾-inch-thick rope, and cut it into ½-inch segments. Roll each segment into a rough ball in your floured hands. Press and roll each segment down the curved side of a fork to make a ridged gnocco with an indentation on one side. Repeat with the remaining dough.

Bring a large pot of salted water to a boil. When it's boiling, add the gnocchi. As soon as the gnocchi have gone into the water, set a large skillet over medium heat and melt the butter. Once the butter is sizzling, add the cream and a ladle-full of pasta water. Bring this mixture to a boil. Simmer until it's reduced by almost half, 3 to 4 minutes. Stir the gnocchi, and simmer until they're cooked through, 5 to 7 minutes from the time they rise to the surface.

Scoop the gnocchi out of the water with a spider strainer, and add them to the simmering sauce. Add the Gorgonzola. Toss to coat them in the sauce, adding a little pasta water if it seems dry. Off heat, sprinkle with the grated Grana Padano, toss, and serve immediately.

Timballo with Sausage Ragù

Timballo al Ragù di Salsiccie

Serves 8

FOR THE SAUSAGE RAGÙ

1 small onion, coarsely chopped

1 small carrot, coarsely chopped

1 stalk celery, coarsely chopped

2 garlic cloves, crushed and peeled

2 tablespoons extra-virgin olive oil

1 pound sweet Italian sausage, removed from casings

Kosher salt

¼ teaspoon peperoncino flakes

½ cup dry white wine

One 28-ounce can whole San Marzano tomatoes, crushed by hand

2 fresh bay leaves

1 cup frozen peas

FOR ASSEMBLY

Kosher salt

2 tablespoons unsalted butter, plus more for the baking pan

¼ cup plus 2 tablespoons fine dried bread crumbs

1 pound ditalini

1¼ cups freshly grated Grana Padano

1 cup cubed prosciutto cotto or other ham

1 cup cubed provola

Timballo, an Italian pasta dish baked in a mold, usually includes additional ingredients such as boiled eggs, meats, vegetables, and cheese to bind it all. Once baked, it is inverted and presented like a cake. Just about every region of Italy has some form of the timballo, including bomba, pasticcio, and, in Naples, sartù. It is usually served during the holidays, but I think making it simpler, with a sausage ragù, gives you a festive presentation for an everyday meal that everyone will love. I am sure most of you recall the iconic timballo served in the movie *Big Night*. Well, here is a version of it.

For the ragù: Combine the onion, carrot, celery, and garlic in a food processor, and pulse to make a fine paste or pestata. Heat the olive oil in a medium Dutch oven over medium heat. When the oil is hot, add the pestata, and cook, stirring often, until it is dried out and sticks to the bottom of the pot, 5 to 6 minutes. Crumble in the sausage, and cook, breaking it up with a wooden spoon, until it's finely crumbled and lightly browned, about 4 minutes. Season with 1 teaspoon salt and the peperoncino.

Add the white wine, and adjust the heat to simmer and reduce the liquid by half, about 2 minutes. Add the tomatoes, bay leaves, and 2 cups water. Cook until it's very thick and flavorful, about 15 to 20 minutes; add the peas in the last 2 to 3 minutes of cooking time. You should have about 5 cups sauce. (If you have less, you can add a little bit of water; if much more, reserve the extra for another use.) Remove the bay leaves and garlic and discard them.

To assemble: Bring a large pot of salted water to a boil. Generously butter a 9-inch springform pan. Sprinkle 2 tablespoons of the bread crumbs in the pan, and shake to coat the bottom and sides thoroughly in the crumb mixture. Preheat the oven to 400 degrees.

Add the ditalini to the boiling water, and cook only until the pasta is still very al dente, 3 to 4 minutes shy of the package directions. →

← Drain it in a colander, and cool it under cold running water. Shake the colander to dry everything off as much as possible.

Add the pasta to the sausage ragù with 1 cup of the grated Grana Padano, and stir. Stir in the ham and provola, distributing them evenly.

Transfer the mixture to the prepared pan, and press the mixture down to compact it slightly. (If you have a cup or so of dressed pasta left over, that's okay—it's the cook's treat!) Sprinkle the top with the remaining ¼ cup each bread crumbs and Grana Padano, and dot the top with the butter. Bake on a rimmed baking sheet, to catch any drips, until the top is very browned and crusty, 40 to 45 minutes. Cool on a rack for 15 to 20 minutes (it will still be quite warm). Run a thin paring knife around the edges of the pan to loosen the timballo, unmold it, and serve.

Spaghetti in Lemon Cream Sauce

Spaghetti al Limone

Serves 6

Kosher salt

1 pound spaghetti

6 tablespoons unsalted butter

Finely grated zest of 1 lemon, plus juice of 2 lemons

¼ teaspoon peperoncino flakes

1 cup heavy cream

1 cup freshly grated Grana Padano

When I was opening up my first restaurant in New York in the early 1970s, everyone wanted fettuccine Alfredo—a much heavier and richer dish than this one, but it always reminded me of this close ancestor from Italy. Lemons from the Amalfi coast and Sorrento area have a particularly fragrant rind, a lot of pulp, and juice high in acidity. They are used most often to make the liqueur limoncello, but in this recipe, the acidity of the lemons cuts into the fat of the cream a bit, making a very balanced dish. The lemony flavor is like a bite of summer in your mouth. If you have been to the Amalfi coast, the home of the *limoni sorrentini,* you've surely had this delicious dish, and wondered how it can be so simple and so tasty. Well, here is the recipe.

Bring a large pot of salted water to a boil for the spaghetti. Add the spaghetti to the water when you're ready to start the sauce.

For the sauce: Melt the butter in a skillet over medium heat. Once it begins to foam, add the lemon zest and peperoncino. Let the zest sizzle for a minute; then add the lemon juice, and bring it to a boil. Add the cream and 1 teaspoon salt, and bring the liquid to a simmer to thicken it slightly, 1 to 2 minutes.

Once the spaghetti is al dente, remove it with tongs to the simmering sauce and add about ½ cup pasta water. Toss to coat the pasta in the sauce, and let it simmer a minute to thicken the sauce and coat the spaghetti, adding a little pasta water if needed.

Remove the skillet from the heat, and sprinkle with the grated cheese. Toss it, and serve.

Bucatini with Broccoli Walnut Pesto

Bucatini al Pesto di Broccoli e Noci

Serves 6

Kosher salt

2 stalks broccoli, cut into florets
(about 4 heaping cups)

½ cup walnut halves, toasted

1 cup packed fresh Italian
parsley leaves

1 cup packed fresh basil leaves

2 garlic cloves, crushed and peeled

Peperoncino flakes

½ cup extra-virgin olive oil

½ cup freshly grated Grana Padano

1 pound bucatini

The deep, rich flavor of this broccoli-walnut pesto reminds me of fall. In our supermarkets today, we find most vegetables and nuts all year long, but that was not so when I was growing up. Broccoli is a winter vegetable, and walnuts mature in the fall and were plentiful in the winter. The pesto is easy to make in a food processor. When it's tossed with the hot bucatini, it makes a dish that will warm your insides and feel like a loving hug.

Bring a large pot of salted water to a boil. Prepare a bowl of ice water. Add the broccoli florets to the boiling water, and cook until they're just tender, about 4 minutes. Remove them to the bowl of ice water to cool. Drain them, and pat them dry. Return the water to a boil for the pasta.

Put the broccoli in a food processor with the walnuts, parsley, basil, garlic, 1 teaspoon salt, and a big pinch of peperoncino. Pulse to make a chunky paste. With the processor running, add the olive oil in a slow, steady stream, to make a smooth and bright-green pesto. Scrape it into a large serving bowl, and stir in the grated cheese.

Add the pasta to the water, and cook until it's al dente. When the pasta is cooked, remove it with tongs to the bowl with the pesto. Add ½ cup pasta-cooking water, and toss well to coat the pasta with the pesto, adding a little more pasta water if it seems dry.

Spicy Lobster Linguine

Linguine all'Aragosta con Sugo Piccante

Serves 6

Kosher salt

6 lobster tails, halved lengthwise

All-purpose flour, for dredging

Vegetable oil, for frying the lobster

¼ cup extra-virgin olive oil, plus more for drizzling

1 large onion, chopped

3 garlic cloves, crushed and peeled

½ cup dry white wine

One 28-ounce can whole San Marzano tomatoes, crushed by hand

3 fresh bay leaves

1 teaspoon dried oregano, preferably Sicilian oregano on the branch

½ teaspoon peperoncino flakes

1 pound linguine

¼ cup chopped fresh Italian parsley

This recipe calls for lobster tails, because they're easier to handle and available frozen year-round, but I also love making the sauce with whole Maine lobsters. If you want to try it that way, separate the claws and small legs from the bodies of three lobsters. Remove and halve the tails, halve the heads and bodies, and clean out the head and the digestive tract that runs along the back. Proceed to flour and fry and make the sauce as described in the recipe. Add the claws and legs a few minutes before you add the rest of the lobster to the sauce. If you use whole lobsters, put a big bowl in the middle of the table for your family to throw the shells into. It is quite a bit of fun to see everyone working through the lobster with their hands, getting all the meat out, fingers dirty. I taught my children and my grandchildren how to eat whole lobsters so not a tiny bit gets wasted, going through each piece with care.

Bring a large pot of salted water to a boil for the pasta.

Season the cut sides of the lobster with ½ teaspoon salt. Spread some flour on a plate, and dredge the cut sides of the lobster lightly in flour.

Heat about ¼ inch of vegetable oil in a large Dutch oven over medium-high heat. Sear the lobster pieces all over, removing them to a plate as they brown. Pour out the oil, and wipe the Dutch oven clean.

Return the Dutch oven to medium heat, and add the olive oil. When the oil is hot, add the onion and garlic. Add a ladle-full of pasta water, and cook until the onion is tender, about 8 minutes. Add the white wine, and reduce it by half, about 1 minute. Add the tomatoes, bay leaves, 1 teaspoon salt, the oregano, and the peperoncino. Rinse out the tomato can with 1 cup pasta water, and add that as well. Bring the liquid to a simmer, and cook until the sauce is thickened, about 10 to 15 minutes. Add the tail pieces, and simmer until they are cooked through, about 3 minutes. Remove the tails to a medium skillet or saucepan with about 1 cup sauce, and keep them warm over very low heat (you don't want to cook the →

← lobster any more, just keep it warm). Remove and discard the garlic cloves and bay leaves.

Meanwhile, add the pasta to the boiling water, and stir. When the pasta is al dente, remove it with tongs to the simmering sauce. Sprinkle with the parsley, and drizzle with a little olive oil. Toss to coat the pasta in the sauce. Serve the pasta with the lobster on top, and drizzle with any remaining sauce.

Spaghetti with Mixed Spring Vegetables

Spaghetti Primavera

Serves 6

Kosher salt

2 tablespoons extra-virgin olive oil

2 tablespoons unsalted butter

2 cups sliced mixed mushrooms
(button, cremini, shiitake, oyster, etc.)

1 cup diced zucchini

3 ripe plum tomatoes, seeded
and diced (about 1½ cups)

2 garlic cloves, finely chopped

Peperoncino flakes

¾ cup heavy cream

1 pound spaghetti

½ bunch medium-thick asparagus,
tough ends trimmed, lower thirds
peeled, stalks cut into 2-inch lengths

1 cup 2-inch pieces
trimmed green beans

1 cup frozen peas

½ cup fresh basil leaves, shredded

½ cup freshly grated Grana Padano

I always encourage you to change my recipes if there's an ingredient you don't like in them, and this is a perfect time to do just that. You can add other spring vegetables, such as scallions, and omit others—for example, if your family aren't fans of mushrooms. When you make substitutions, it's important to take into consideration the cooking times of all the different vegetables you are adding, so that one isn't over- or undercooked.

Bring a large pot of salted water to a boil for the pasta.

Heat a large skillet over medium-high heat. Add the olive oil and butter. Once the butter is melted, add the mushrooms and zucchini. Cook until they're wilted and lightly browned on the underside, about 2 minutes. Toss, and brown the second side, about 2 minutes more. Add the tomatoes and garlic, and cook until the tomatoes begin to give up their juices, about 3 minutes. Season with 1 teaspoon salt and a big pinch of peperoncino. Add the cream and ½ cup pasta water, and simmer while you cook the pasta.

Add the spaghetti to the boiling water. When the spaghetti is about halfway cooked, add the asparagus, green beans, and peas. Cook until the pasta is al dente and the vegetables are just tender. Remove with a spider strainer to the simmering sauce. Toss to coat the pasta in the sauce, adding a little more pasta water if it seems dry. Add the basil, toss, and remove from the heat. Sprinkle with the grated cheese, toss, and serve immediately.

Fettuccine with Caramelized Onions, Bacon, and Olives

Fettuccine con Cipolle, Pancetta e Olive

Serves 6

Kosher salt

2 tablespoons extra-virgin olive oil

4 ounces slab bacon, cut into lardons

2 large onions, sliced (about 4 cups)

1 tablespoon chopped fresh thyme

2 teaspoons balsamic vinegar

2 tablespoons tomato paste

½ cup pitted Gaeta olives, coarsely chopped

½ cup dry white wine

1 pound fettucine

¼ cup chopped fresh Italian parsley

½ cup freshly grated Grana Padano

When I was growing up, we always had a slab of bacon or pancetta hanging in the *cantina,* and even in my early years in the United States, there was always some in the refrigerator. A little piece in soup or a pasta sauce added a lot of flavor and went a long way.

Take your time making this sauce. The caramelization of the onions is key and will add a layer of complexity to the dish. Let them turn a deep golden brown. Let the bacon crisp. The few extra minutes of attention will add to the flavor tenfold. The briny olives complement these other two flavors beautifully.

Bring a large pot of salted water to a boil for the pasta.

Heat a large skillet over medium heat. Add the olive oil and bacon. Cook until the bacon is just crisp, about 4 minutes. Spoon off all but ¼ cup fat from the pan, and add the onions. Season with 1 teaspoon salt, and reduce the heat to medium low. Cook until the onions are wilted, about 10 minutes. Add the thyme and vinegar, and continue to cook until the onions are deep golden, stirring often so they don't burn, 10 to 15 minutes more.

Increase the heat to medium. Make a space in the pan, and add the tomato paste to that spot. Cook and stir the tomato paste there for a minute, until it darkens a shade or two. Add the olives, and stir everything together. Add the white wine, bring to a simmer, and cook until the liquid is reduced by half, 1 to 2 minutes. Add 1½ cups pasta water, and simmer it while you cook the pasta.

Add the pasta to the boiling water. When it is al dente, remove the pasta with tongs directly to the sauce. Add the parsley, bring to a simmer, and toss to coat the pasta in the sauce, adding a little pasta water if it seems dry. Season with salt if needed. Remove the skillet from the heat, and sprinkle with the grated cheese. Toss, and serve.

Penne Rigate with Sausage, Mushrooms, and Ricotta

Penne Rigate con Salsiccia, Funghi e Ricotta

Serves 6

Kosher salt

3 tablespoons extra-virgin olive oil

8 ounces sweet Italian sausages, removed from casings

1 medium onion, finely chopped

12 ounces mixed wild mushrooms (such as button, cremini, oyster, shiitake, chanterelle), thickly sliced

4 ripe plum tomatoes, seeded and diced

2 teaspoons chopped fresh thyme

Peperoncino flakes

2 cups low-sodium chicken stock

1 pound penne

¼ cup chopped fresh Italian parsley

1 cup good-quality fresh ricotta

½ cup freshly grated Grana Padano

This recipe will become a regular request from your family and guests. It is often known as *boscaiola,* or "of the forest," because of the earthy mushrooms in the sauce. Definitely one of Tanya's favorites, this dish spent many years on the menus of my restaurants. On cold winter nights in New York City, when Tanya and her teenage friends had no other place to go, I would serve them this pasta followed by hot chocolate in our private dining room. I loved seeing them so full, chatty, and happy. It is easy to assemble, flavorful, and filling.

Bring a large pot of salted water to a boil for the pasta.

Heat a large skillet over medium heat and add the olive oil. When the oil is hot, crumble in the sausages, and break them up with a wooden spoon into fine crumbles. Cook until the sausage is no longer pink, 3 to 4 minutes. Add the onion, and cook until it begins to soften, about 4 minutes. Stir in the mushrooms, cover, and cook until they release their liquid, 3 to 4 minutes.

Uncover, and increase the heat to reduce away any liquid left in the pot. Add the tomatoes and thyme. Season with 1 teaspoon salt and a pinch of peperoncino. Cook until the tomatoes just begin to break down, about 2 minutes. Add the stock, and bring to a simmer. Cover, and cook until the texture becomes saucy, about 10 minutes. Uncover, and increase the heat to thicken the sauce slightly, 1 to 2 minutes.

Meanwhile, cook the penne in the boiling water until it's al dente. When the penne is done, remove with a spider strainer directly to the sauce, and add the parsley. Toss to coat the pasta with the sauce, adding a little more pasta water if it seems dry. Remove the pot from the heat, add the ricotta and grated cheese, toss, and serve.

Rigatoni with Turkey Meatballs

Rigatoni con Polpette di Tacchino

Serves 6

1 small onion, cut into chunks

1 small carrot, cut into chunks

1 stalk celery, cut into chunks

½ cup fresh Italian parsley leaves

2 garlic cloves, crushed and peeled

1 pound ground turkey (93/7)

1 large egg, beaten

¾ cup freshly grated Grana Padano

½ cup fine dried bread crumbs

Kosher salt

3 tablespoons extra-virgin olive oil

One 28-ounce can whole
San Marzano tomatoes,
crushed by hand

1 teaspoon dried oregano, preferably
Sicilian oregano on the branch

Peperoncino flakes

1 pound rigatoni

½ cup fresh basil leaves, shredded

Pasta and meatballs is an Italian American classic. You won't find it in Italy. Italian immigrants added meat to their sauce to enhance the tomatoes they found in America, which had less flavor than those grown under the Vesuvius volcano. In Italy, meatballs are eaten separately from pasta. Pasta with meatballs was on the menus of my early restaurants, and I really grew to love it. When my kids were in school, for Family Food Day, you brought in an ethnic dish. I initially sent in something traditional, like a pasticciata, but what the kids really all wanted was meatballs.

Preheat the oven to 450 degrees, and line a baking sheet with parchment.

Combine the onion, carrot, celery, parsley, and garlic in a food processor. Pulse to make a smooth paste or pestata. Scrape half of the pestata into a large bowl, and reserve the rest. To the bowl, add the turkey, egg, ½ cup of the grated cheese, the bread crumbs, and 1 teaspoon salt. Mix well with your hands, form it into eighteen meatballs, and place them on the prepared baking sheet. Bake until the meatballs are firm (they don't have to be totally cooked through at this point), about 10 minutes.

Heat a large Dutch oven over medium heat. Add the olive oil. When the oil is hot, add the reserved pestata and cook, stirring occasionally, until it begins to dry out, about 3 minutes. Add the tomatoes and 3 cups water. Add the oregano, and season with 1 teaspoon salt and a big pinch of peperoncino. Simmer while the meatballs bake, about 10 minutes.

Add the baked meatballs to the sauce, and cook until the sauce is thick and flavorful, about 20 minutes.

Meanwhile, bring a large pot of salted water to a boil. Add the pasta, and cook until it's al dente. While the pasta cooks, remove the meatballs to a shallow serving bowl and top them with a cup or two of the sauce. When the pasta is al dente, remove it with a spider strainer to the Dutch oven with the simmering sauce. Add the basil, and toss to coat the pasta with the sauce, adding a little of the pasta water if it seems dry. Remove from the heat, sprinkle with the remaining grated Grana Padano, and serve with the meatballs on top.

Rigatoni with Sausage and Cabbage

Rigatoni con Salsiccia e Verza

Serves 6

Kosher salt

3 tablespoons extra-virgin olive oil

3 sweet Italian sausages (totaling about 12 ounces), removed from casings

1 large red onion, sliced

2 teaspoons chopped fresh thyme

1 small head savoy cabbage, coarsely shredded

Peperoncino flakes

3 tablespoons tomato paste

1 pound rigatoni

1 cup freshly grated Grana Padano

When I was a young girl, my grandma and grandpa raised pigs, and they would ask the traveling town butcher to come and assist them with the slaughter and the butchering, so that every single part of each animal would be put to good use. From the pig came prosciutto, pancetta, lard, head cheese, and sausage, among other things. The sausages were hung with great care next to the prosciutto in the *cantina,* and in the winter months they made the best accompaniment to cabbage for a simple and easy pasta dish. This is a great winter pasta recipe. It is easy and flavorful and combines pasta, meat, and veggies in one dish. If you are worried about kids and cabbage, just cut the cabbage thinner and let it cook longer in the sauce; it will break down, almost disappearing into the sauce, and make it creamier—the kids won't notice the veggies but will love the taste.

Bring a large pot of salted water to a boil for the pasta.

Heat a large Dutch oven over medium heat, and add the olive oil. When the oil is hot, crumble in the sausage. Breaking it up with a wooden spoon, cook until the sausage is browned, about 5 minutes.

Add the red onion and thyme. Stir and cook until the onion begins to wilt, about 4 minutes. Stir in the cabbage, and season with 1 teaspoon salt and a pinch of peperoncino. Cook until the cabbage begins to brown and wilt, 5 to 6 minutes. Make a space in the pan, and add the tomato paste to that spot. Cook and stir the tomato paste there for a minute, until it darkens a shade or two; then stir it into the cabbage. Add 2 cups pasta water, and bring the liquid to a simmer. Cover, and cook until the cabbage is very tender, 20 to 25 minutes. Uncover, and bring the sauce to a rapid simmer to thicken it slightly, if needed, about 2 minutes.

When the cabbage is almost done, add the pasta to the boiling water and cook until it's al dente. Add it to the simmering sauce. Toss to coat the pasta with the sauce, adding a little pasta water if it seems dry. Remove from the heat, sprinkle with the grated cheese, toss, and serve.

Spaghetti with Roasted Cherry Tomato Sauce

Spaghetti con Pomodorini al Forno

Serves 6

1¼ cups grated pecorino

½ cup panko bread crumbs

¼ cup chopped fresh Italian parsley

⅓ cup plus 2 tablespoons extra-virgin olive oil

3 cups halved cherry or grape tomatoes

2 garlic cloves, sliced

Kosher salt

Peperoncino flakes

1 pound spaghetti

½ cup chopped fresh basil

If you travel through southern Italy during the summer you are bound to find some rendition of this dish in every town. Delicious and simple to assemble, it will become one of your favorites, I am sure. Tanya and I discovered racks and racks of tomatoes drying in the sun, their sugars intensifying, while filming my public television show in Italy. We ate pasta with those tomatoes almost every day we were there, and have brought the tradition home with us. If you don't have a garden or terrace to dry your tomatoes in the sun, baking them is a flavorful alternative.

Preheat the oven to 400 degrees. Line 2 baking sheets with parchment.

In a large bowl, toss together 1 cup of the pecorino, the panko, and the parsley. Drizzle with ⅓ cup of the oil and toss well. Add the tomatoes, garlic, 1 teaspoon salt, and a pinch of peperoncino. Toss well to coat the tomatoes in the crumb mixture.

Scatter the tomatoes on the baking sheets, scraping any excess crumbs from the bowl on top of them. Bake until the tomatoes are shriveled but still juicy and the crumbs are crisp and golden, 25 to 30 minutes, tossing once halfway through.

When the tomatoes are almost done, bring a large pot of salted water to a boil for the pasta. Add the spaghetti to the boiling water and cook until it is al dente.

Transfer the hot cooked tomatoes to a large serving bowl. Drain the pasta with tongs, and add it directly to the bowl with the remaining ¼ cup pecorino and the basil. Drizzle with the remaining 2 tablespoons olive oil, and add a ladle or two of pasta water. Toss well, adding a little more pasta water if it still seems dry.

Four-Cheese Baked Macaroni

Pasta al Forno ai Quattro Formaggi

Serves 8

6 tablespoons unsalted butter, plus more for the baking dish

Kosher salt

2-to-3-ounce chunk of day-old country bread, crust removed

½ cup freshly grated Grana Padano

¼ cup all-purpose flour

3½ cups whole milk

2 fresh bay leaves

8 ounces Italian Fontina, grated

8 ounces mild provola, grated

4 ounces Taleggio, rind removed, cut into pieces

1 pound penne

1 small bunch thick asparagus spears, tough ends removed, lower stalks peeled, stalks cut into 1-inch segments

1 cup frozen peas

When I was raising my kids in America, they always asked me about macaroni and cheese at friends' houses. When I looked into it as a young mother, I realized the options were mostly mushy pasta with powdered processed cheese. Mac and cheese has now come a long way from the early 1970s, but back then I came up with my own version for my kids, an elegant Italian rendition; the addition of some asparagus and peas makes it lighter and even more Italian. Their friends really loved my version, and it has stuck.

Preheat the oven to 400 degrees. Butter a 9-by-13-inch baking dish, and set it aside. Bring a large pot of salted water to a boil for the pasta.

Grate (on the large holes of a box grater) the bread into small crumbs; you should have about 1 cup. Melt 2 tablespoons of the butter in a small skillet over medium-low heat. Scatter in the crumbs, and cook, tossing frequently, until they're light golden and crisp, about 3 minutes. Set them aside, and when they're cool, stir in the Grana Padano.

To make the sauce: Melt the remaining 4 tablespoons butter in a large Dutch oven over medium heat. Once the butter is melted, whisk in the flour, and cook to toast it a bit, 1 to 2 minutes. Gradually whisk in the milk until the mixture is smooth. Add the bay leaves and 1 teaspoon salt. Bring to a simmer, and cook, stirring occasionally, until it's thickened, 6 to 8 minutes. Reduce the heat to low, and stir in the Fontina, provola, and Taleggio, a few handfuls at a time, stirring until it's smooth.

Meanwhile, add the pasta to the boiling water. Once the pasta is halfway cooked, add the asparagus and peas, and cook until the pasta is al dente. Drain the pasta and vegetables, and add them directly to the sauce. Stir to coat the pasta thoroughly, and transfer the entire mixture to the prepared baking dish. Sprinkle with the crumbs. Bake until the edges are bubbly and the top is golden brown, 40 to 45 minutes.

Breakfast Pasta Frittata

Frittata di Pasta per Colazione

Serves 4

3 tablespoons extra-virgin olive oil

8 ounces sweet Italian sausage, removed from casings

1 medium red bell pepper, seeded, chopped

1 bunch scallions, chopped

Kosher salt

1 cup grated Italian Fontina

¼ cup freshly grated Grana Padano

6 large eggs

½ cup milk or half-and-half

Freshly ground black pepper

¼ cup chopped fresh Italian parsley

8 ounces spaghetti or other long pasta, cooked, cooled

I am all about reusing or recycling food. Last night's leftover pasta is perfect for this breakfast pasta frittata. Since I know leftover pasta is not a common occurrence in my household, I often make pasta specifically for this recipe. You can feel free to add in any leftover vegetables you might have around as well.

Preheat the oven to 400 degrees.

Heat a medium nonstick skillet over medium heat, and add 1 tablespoon of the oil. When the oil is hot, crumble in the sausage, and cook, breaking it up with a wooden spoon, until it's no longer pink, about 3 minutes. Add the bell pepper, and cook until it's just tender, about 5 minutes. Add the scallions, and cook until they're wilted, about 2 minutes. Season with ½ teaspoon salt. Set this mixture aside. Combine the Fontina and Grana Padano in a small bowl, and toss to combine them.

In a large bowl, combine the eggs and milk or half-and-half, and season with 1 teaspoon salt and several grinds of pepper. Whisk until the mixture is smooth. Stir in half of the cheese mixture and the parsley.

Return the skillet to medium heat. Add the remaining 2 tablespoons olive oil to the sausage-and-pepper mixture. Add the spaghetti, and toss to combine everything. Pour in the egg mixture, and let it cook until the bottom and sides are just set, about 4 minutes. Sprinkle the remaining cheese mixture over the top.

Bake until the frittata is brown and crispy on top and cooked through, 15 to 18 minutes. Let it cool for 10 minutes before removing it from the skillet. Cut it into wedges, and serve warm or at room temperature.

Visiting Nonna Rosa's sister Anna's family in Sunbury, Pennsylvania, 1966

FISH AND SHELLFISH

Istria, where I grew up, is a peninsula surrounded by the Adriatic. Therefore, fish was a staple in our kitchen. But the best fish was expensive, and although we had a fisherman in our house, Uncle Emilio, we mostly ate the secondary choices or less expensive fish, lots of sardines, mackerel, whiting—while the choice fishes went to market. But when the calamari were in season and abundant, or octopus was plentiful, or crabs, we had our fill. Grandma Erminia, although she was not a big fish-lover, cooked all of the other fishes regularly for us.

Stuffed Calamari in Tomato Sauce   133

Turbot Woodsman-Style   135

Fillet of Sole in Lemon Sauce   136

Seafood Salad   139

Halibut Baked in Parchment Paper   140

Marinated Monkfish Medallions   141

Cuttlefish Salad with Potatoes and Olives   142

Manila Clams Triestina   145

Mussels in Red Sauce with Linguine   146

Grouper in Crazy Water   147

Baked Fresh Sardines   148

Stuffed Calamari in Tomato Sauce

Calamari Ripieni in Sugo di Pomodoro

Serves 6

FOR THE CALAMARI

4 ounces small shrimp, peeled, deveined, finely chopped

2 pounds medium calamari, cleaned, with tentacles (about 18 tubes), tentacles finely chopped

½ cup fine dried bread crumbs

¼ cup chopped fresh Italian parsley

¼ teaspoon ground cayenne

Kosher salt

6 tablespoons extra-virgin olive oil

FOR THE SAUCE

2 tablespoons extra-virgin olive oil

4 garlic cloves, sliced

1 cup dry white wine

3½ cups cherry or grape tomatoes, halved

1 teaspoon dried oregano, preferably Sicilian oregano on the branch

2 tablespoons chopped fresh Italian parsley

My uncle Emilio was an electrician by profession, but he supplemented his earnings by fishing. He loved fishing, so it was not a hard task for him to go out into the night, and that is when he would catch calamari. He had a *lampara,* a big bowl-like shade with a battery-fueled lightbulb that shone into the water from the back of the boat. If it was early in the night, he would ask my brother, Franco, and me to come along. He would have us drag strips of white cloth in the seawater under the light, and the calamari would float up like puffs of clouds, thinking it was small fishes. My uncle would lasso them in, one by one, with a hook that looked like a small upside-down palm tree. He would flip them into the boat, and one of us would collect them and put them in a container. We had fun watching them as the purple spots on their bodies moved and changed color. Some of them would squirt black ink in self-defense. As the container filled up, I knew that tomorrow's dinner would be stuffed calamari.

For the calamari: Combine the shrimp, calamari tentacles, bread crumbs, parsley, and cayenne in a large bowl. Season with ½ teaspoon salt. Drizzle with 2 tablespoons of the olive oil, and toss well to coat everything with the oil. Toss to make a stuffing that will clump together loosely in your hand. (If it's still sandy in texture, add a little more oil or a splash of white wine.)

Snip a tiny piece from the pointy end of each calamari tube to make a slightly larger hole (this will make the tubes a little easier to stuff). Fill each calamari tube loosely with stuffing, and close with a toothpick.

Heat a large skillet over medium heat. Add the remaining ¼ cup of the olive oil. When the oil is hot, add the calamari (in batches, if necessary), and brown on all sides, about 5 minutes per batch. Remove them to a plate as they brown.

Once all of the calamari are out, make the sauce: Add the 2 tablespoons olive oil to the pan. Add the garlic, and cook until it's sizzling, about →

← 1 minute. Pour in the wine, and bring the liquid to a simmer, scraping the pan with a wooden spoon to loosen the brown bits from the bottom. Add the tomatoes, oregano, and 1 cup water. Bring to a rapid simmer, and cook until the tomatoes break down slightly to form a sauce, 5 to 10 minutes.

Add the calamari in one layer. Simmer until they are cooked through and turn white, 5 to 10 minutes more. Stir in the parsley, and serve.

Turbot Woodsman-Style

Rombo alla Boscaiola

Serves 4

4 turbot fillets (about 6 ounces each)

Kosher salt

All-purpose flour, for dredging

6 tablespoons extra-virgin olive oil

1 large onion, sliced

10 ounces cremini mushrooms, thickly sliced

10 ounces button mushrooms, thickly sliced

3 stalks celery, chopped

½ cup dry white wine

2 cups tomato passata or hand-crushed canned tomatoes

2 tablespoons chopped fresh Italian parsley

In Italian food culture, fish and mushrooms aren't often thought of as going together. But this is one of my favorite ways of serving up firm white fish. If you can't get turbot, use another firm white fish fillet, such as halibut or sea bass. You can even use cod, though it will require a gentler hand in cooking. This easy and flavorful dish is quick to make. It's delicious served with polenta or rice.

Season the turbot on both sides with 1 teaspoon salt. Spread some flour on a plate, and dredge the fish on both sides in the flour.

Heat a large nonstick skillet over medium heat, and add 4 tablespoons of the olive oil. Add the fish, and cook until it's browned on one side, 2 to 3 minutes. Carefully flip and brown the other side, about 2 minutes. Remove the fish to a plate, and wipe the skillet clean.

Return the skillet to medium heat, and add the remaining 2 tablespoons olive oil. Add the onion, mushrooms, and celery. Season with ½ teaspoon salt. Cook, tossing occasionally, until the vegetables have wilted down; then increase the heat to reduce away any liquid in the pan and brown the mushrooms slightly, about 8 minutes.

Add the wine, and bring it to a simmer to reduce by half. Add the tomatoes and 1½ cups water, and simmer rapidly until the sauce is thickened, about 10 minutes.

Stir in the parsley. Add the fish back to the sauce, and simmer to heat it through and finish cooking, 2 to 4 minutes depending on thickness. Serve immediately.

Fillet of Sole in Lemon Sauce

Filetto di Sogliola al Limone

Serves 4

¼ cup extra-virgin olive oil

Cornstarch, for dredging

4 sole fillets (about 1½ pounds)

Kosher salt

2 garlic cloves, sliced

¼ cup lemon juice, plus 1 lemon, thinly sliced, seeds removed

3 tablespoons capers in brine, drained

½ cup dry white wine

6 scallions, chopped

2 tablespoons unsalted butter, cut into pieces

¼ cup chopped fresh Italian parsley

Fillet of sole is something that most people like even if they do not like fish. It was not a fish I knew growing up; I became familiar with a similar fish, flounder, when opening my first restaurant in New York. It was always on the menu, and was a favorite of my kids when we went out to eat. Fillet of sole is light, and so easy to prepare, and it cooks quickly. It is soft and it breaks easily in the pan, but if you fold the fillet in half, it will be easier to flip. Always use a fish spatula to do so.

Heat the olive oil in a large nonstick skillet over medium heat. Spread a thin layer of cornstarch on a plate. Season the sole with salt, and dredge lightly in the cornstarch. If the fillets are large (or particularly thin), fold them in half before dredging. When the oil is hot, add the fish, and brown on both sides, about 2 minutes per side. Gently remove to a plate.

Add the garlic. Once the garlic is sizzling, add the lemon slices. Cook until the slices are browned, then flip and brown the second side. Add the capers, let them sizzle for a few seconds, and pour in the white wine and lemon juice. Bring the liquid to a boil to reduce by half, about 1 minute; then add 1 cup water. Simmer just until the sauce comes together, about 2 minutes.

Stir in the scallions. Whisk the butter and parsley into the sauce, and add the fish back in, just to warm it through. Serve the fish on warm plates, spooning the sauce over it.

Seafood Salad

Insalata di Mare

Serves 6

Kosher salt

12 ounces green beans, trimmed

2 lemons, peels julienned, juiced (¼ cup juice)

1 cup dry white wine

1 stalk celery, coarsely chopped, plus 4 inner celery stalks, sliced, with some leaves

1 medium carrot, coarsely chopped

3 fresh bay leaves

1 pound medium calamari, tubes and tentacles, tubes cut into ½-inch rings

1 pound large shrimp, peeled, deveined

2 pounds mussels, scrubbed

2 cups cherry or grape tomatoes, halved

¼ cup red wine vinegar

½ cup extra-virgin olive oil

¼ teaspoon peperoncino flakes

½ cup chopped fresh Italian parsley

In the early days of Felidia, we had a green marble table in the front of the dining room with a large antipasto display, including such dishes as caprese salad, grilled vegetables, and sliced prosciutto and melon. There was also seafood salad with the freshest fish or shellfish we had found at the market that morning. There are many versions of seafood salad; here I have taken the traditional combination and lightened and stretched it a bit by adding some cooked string beans and lemon rind as well as some grape tomatoes.

Bring 3 quarts of water to a boil, and season with 2 teaspoons salt. Add the green beans, and simmer for 2 minutes. Add the lemon peel, and simmer until the beans and peel are tender, about 4 minutes more. Remove them with a spider strainer to a colander. Rinse them under cold water until they're chilled. Drain, and pat them dry. Put them in a large serving bowl.

To the same water, add the white wine, and return the liquid to a simmer. Add the chopped celery, the carrot, and the bay leaves. Add the calamari, and simmer until just cooked through, 2 to 3 minutes. Remove the calamari with a spider strainer to the serving bowl. Keep the vegetables in the liquid.

Return the poaching liquid to a simmer, and add the shrimp. Simmer until they're just cooked through, about 4 minutes. Remove them with a spider strainer, and add them to the calamari.

Return the poaching liquid to a simmer again, and add the mussels. Cover the pot, and cook until the mussels open, about 5 minutes, discarding any that do not open. Remove the mussels to a colander. Once they're cool, pluck the mussels from the shells. Add them to the large bowl, along with the sliced celery and the tomatoes. Drizzle with lemon juice, the vinegar, and the oil, and season with 1 teaspoon salt and the peperoncino. Toss well. Add the parsley, toss once more, and serve.

Halibut Baked in Parchment Paper

Ippoglosso al Cartoccio

Serves 4

Kosher salt

1 small fennel bulb, quartered, cored, sliced into ½-inch wedges

1 small red onion, sliced into ½-inch rings

4 slices ripe tomato

2 tablespoons capers in brine, drained

16 black Italian olives, such as Gaeta, pitted

¼ cup chopped fresh Italian parsley

2 tablespoons extra-virgin olive oil

4 skinless halibut fillets (about 6 ounces each)

Freshly ground black pepper to taste

This recipe can easily be doubled or tripled. It is a great fish dish that does not need a lot of attention—perfect when you have dinner guests. You put it in the oven while the guests are having appetizers, and then, with a spatula, set the whole packets straight from the oven onto their plates. Let them open the packets, and the aroma will come steaming out. It makes a big impression when entertaining, and also keeps this fish nice and warm until right before your guests start eating.

Preheat the oven to 450 degrees. Cut four half-sheet-pan-sized pieces of parchment into large hearts, and fold them in half to make a crease in the center of each heart.

Bring a medium saucepan of salted water to a boil. Add the fennel pieces, and simmer until they're crisp-tender, 7 to 8 minutes. Add the onion rings, and simmer just until they begin to wilt, about 1 minute more. Drain the fennel and onion, and rinse to cool them slightly. Pat them dry, and add them to a large bowl. Add the tomato slices, capers, olives, parsley, and ½ teaspoon salt. Drizzle everything with the olive oil, and gently toss to coat.

Lay the parchment hearts out on your work surface. Set a tomato slice on the right side of each heart, near the crease, and evenly distribute the fennel mixture on top of the tomatoes. Top each with a halibut fillet. Season each fillet with salt and pepper. Fold the left side of the parchment heart over. Beginning at the top of the heart, crimp the edges to seal the parchment: make small folds, each one overlapping the last, until you get to the bottom or tip of the heart and turn the last fold under.

Place the packages on a baking sheet, and bake until the parchment is puffed and browned, about 20 minutes, depending on the thickness of the fillets. Serve the packets on plates, taking care when your guests cut them open—they will be very hot.

Marinated Monkfish Medallions

Medaglioni di Rospo in Saor

Serves 4 to 6

2 pounds monkfish fillet, cleaned, cut into 1-to-2-inch chunks

Kosher salt

All-purpose flour, for dredging

6 tablespoons extra-virgin olive oil

1 large onion, sliced

2 garlic cloves, sliced

4 fresh bay leaves

2 sprigs fresh rosemary

1½ cups dry white wine

⅓ cup white wine vinegar

½ cup golden raisins

¼ cup pine nuts, toasted

Saor is a traditional preparation in Istria and the Veneto. Sailors would prepare the fish in this fashion while at sea, and it kept for days. Sardines were the typical fish my mother would make in saor, but I love the texture and flavor of monkfish, and it keeps firm for several days, even a week, in the marinade of lots of onions and vinegar. Great as either an appetizer or a main course, it also is wonderful on buffet tables.

This dish was traditionally made with bluefish, sardines, or mackerel, because they were cheaper and more abundant fish. You can make it with those and it will be delicious, but I use monkfish—which was highly prized in Italy, and made in saor only on special occasions.

Season the monkfish with 1 teaspoon salt. Spread some flour in a shallow bowl for dredging. Heat about 4 tablespoons of the olive oil in a large nonstick skillet over medium heat. Lightly dredge the monkfish pieces in flour, and fry them in the oil in two batches until they're cooked through and crisp and golden all over, 5 to 6 minutes per batch. Drain on a paper-towel-lined baking sheet.

Add the remaining 2 tablespoons olive oil to the skillet. When the oil is hot, add the onion, and cook until it's tender and lightly browned, about 8 minutes. Add the garlic, bay leaves, and rosemary, and season with ½ teaspoon salt. Add the wine and vinegar. Bring to a simmer to reduce slightly, 3 to 4 minutes. Add the raisins and pine nuts, and simmer until the liquid is reduced by half, 2 to 3 minutes more.

Layer half of the monkfish in a serving dish where it will fit snugly. Add half of the onion mixture over the top, leaving the liquid, rosemary, and bay leaves behind. Top with the remaining monkfish, spread the remaining onion mixture over the top, and drizzle the liquid from the pan over the top. Cover, and refrigerate for at least 2 hours or up to overnight. Let it return to room temperature before serving.

Cuttlefish Salad with Potatoes and Olives

Insalata di Seppia con Patate e Olive

Serves 6

2 pounds small cuttlefish, cleaned, beaks removed (about 8 pieces)

3 stalks young celery, trimmed, sliced (reserve the trimmings)

2 fresh bay leaves

2 medium russet potatoes

1 small red onion, thinly sliced

¾ cup pitted Gaeta olives

½ cup plus 2 tablespoons extra-virgin olive oil

¼ cup plus 1 tablespoon red wine vinegar

¼ cup chopped fresh Italian parsley

Kosher salt

¼ teaspoon peperoncino flakes

I often ate cuttlefish as a child. It is not usually seen on menus in America, although it is becoming more and more prevalent, and this is a wonderful way to prepare it. Cuttlefish is in the same family as octopus and calamari, and is cooked in much the same fashion. It can be fried, made into a sauce or brodetto, or boiled and made into a salad. I love it in all these preparations, but I love it most dressed as a salad with potatoes. When the cuttlefish are small, I leave them whole. The cuttlefish has a wide, chalky backbone; this is removed when the fish is cleaned, which turns it into a small pocket when cooked. In this case, I make the potato salad separately and use it to stuff the cooked fish. This makes a great presentation, but if you can only get large cuttlefish, boil them, cut them into strips like French fries, and toss them together with the potatoes.

Place the cleaned cuttlefish, celery trimmings, and bay leaves in a pot with water to cover by about 2 inches. Bring to a boil, and reduce the heat so the water is simmering gently. Cook until the cuttlefish is tender but still slightly al dente, about 15 minutes. (Poke it with a fork; if the cuttlefish is cooked, the fork will penetrate easily.) Drain the cuttlefish, and let them cool slightly.

Meanwhile, in a second pot, cover the potatoes with cold water and bring it to a simmer. Simmer until the potatoes are tender, about 20 minutes. Cool until you can handle them; then peel and cube them. Add them to a serving bowl with the sliced celery, red onion, and olives. Drizzle everything with ½ cup olive oil and ¼ cup vinegar, and add the parsley, 1 teaspoon salt, and the peperoncino. Toss well.

Put the cuttlefish in a second bowl. Drizzle with the remaining 2 tablespoons oil, the remaining 1 tablespoon vinegar, and ½ teaspoon salt. Toss to coat the cuttlefish.

Spoon some of the potato mixture into the cavity of each cuttlefish, and arrange them in a circle on a large platter. Spoon the rest of the potato mixture into the center of the platter. Serve immediately.

Manila Clams Triestina

Vongole Veraci alla Triestina

Serves 4

½ cup extra-virgin olive oil

1 medium onion, sliced

4 garlic cloves, sliced

6 scallions, sliced, white and green parts separated

3 fresh bay leaves

4 sprigs fresh thyme

¼ teaspoon peperoncino flakes

2 cups dry white wine

3 pounds Manila clams, soaked, scrubbed clean

½ cup chopped fresh Italian parsley

¼ cup fine dried bread crumbs

Kosher salt

Country bread, grilled, for serving

Trieste is a beautiful seaport city not far from Venice, on the border of what is now Slovenia. In the aftermath of World War II, when Istria was ceded to communist Yugoslavia, quite a few of my relatives moved to Trieste. On our way to America, we were refugees in Campo San Saba, near Trieste, and on Sundays we would visit with Zia Nina and Zio Rapetti. Zio Rapetti would take us to Barcola, where he had a small fishing boat. Surrounding the bay were big rocks, on which the mussels made their home. With a small knife and a pail, we would harvest enough of them for dinner, and Zia Nina would make them in this traditional style. I love clams, so I use the same recipe to make clams triestina, but you can use either clams or mussels in this recipe.

Heat 4 tablespoons of the olive oil in a large Dutch oven over medium heat. Add the onion, and cook until it's just golden around the edges, 4 to 5 minutes. Add the garlic, scallion whites, bay leaves, thyme, and ¼ teaspoon peperoncino. Cook until everything is sizzling, about 1 minute. Pour in the white wine, bring to a boil, and simmer to reduce by half, about 3 to 4 minutes.

Once the wine has reduced, add the clams, drizzle with 2 tablespoons of the oil, and stir. Cover, and simmer until the clams open, about 5 minutes. When most of the clams have opened, discard any that have not. Sprinkle with the parsley, scallion greens, and bread crumbs, and bring to a boil so the bread crumbs can thicken the sauce. Taste the broth, and season with salt (clams can sometimes be salty, so you might not need much). Drizzle with the remaining 2 tablespoons olive oil, and toss well. Transfer the clams to a serving bowl, and pour the juices over the top. Serve immediately with some grilled country bread.

Mussels in Red Sauce with Linguine

Linguine con Cozze e Pomodoro

Serves 6

Kosher salt

½ cup extra-virgin olive oil

6 garlic cloves, sliced

½ cup pitted Taggiasca or Gaeta olives

One 28-ounce can whole San Marzano tomatoes, crushed by hand

2 fresh bay leaves

1 teaspoon dried oregano, preferably Sicilian oregano on the branch

Peperoncino flakes

1 pound linguine

2 pounds fresh mussels in the shell, scrubbed

¼ cup chopped fresh Italian parsley

I grew up on mussels I plucked from the rocks on the Adriatic coast, and ate them mostly in a white wine sauce, sautéed with onions and some parsley. Mussels are loved and appreciated in all of coastal Italy, but mussels in a red sauce and served with pasta is iconic Neapolitan fare. This recipe is easy to make, satisfying, and relatively economical. Using very fresh mussels is essential to the success of this dish. I like to serve it as they do in Naples, with the mussels in their shells. If you have fussy guests, once the mussels are cooked and opened, you can remove them from their shells and return them to the sauce.

Bring a large pot of salted water to a boil for the pasta.

Heat a large Dutch oven over medium heat and add the olive oil. When the oil is hot, add the garlic and olives, and cook until they're sizzling, about 1 minute. Add the tomatoes, rinse out the can with 1 cup pasta water, and add that to the pot. Bring the liquid to a simmer; add the bay leaves, oregano, ½ teaspoon peperoncino, and 1 teaspoon salt. Simmer until the sauce is flavorful and has thickened slightly, about 10 minutes.

Add the linguine to the boiling water.

Add the mussels to the sauce, and return it to a simmer. Cover the pot, and cook until the mussels open, 4 to 5 minutes, discarding any that don't open. Discard the bay leaves.

When the pasta is al dente, remove it with tongs directly to the awaiting sauce. Toss to coat the pasta with the sauce, adding a little of the pasta water if it seems dry.

Remove the pot from the heat. Sprinkle with the parsley. Toss well, and serve.

Grouper in Crazy Water

Cernia all'Acqua Pazza

Serves 4

4 grouper fillets (about 6 to 7 ounces each), plus the bones and heads

6 ripe medium plum tomatoes, cored, quartered

1 lemon, halved

4 garlic cloves, crushed and peeled

3 whole dried peperoncini

4 sprigs fresh Italian parsley

2 fresh bay leaves

1 cup dry white wine

¼ cup extra-virgin olive oil

Kosher salt

¼ cup capers in brine, drained

½ cup Taggiasca olives, pitted

4 scallions, chopped, white and green parts separated

¾ cup ditalini or other small pasta shape

Acqua Pazza (literally, "Crazy Water") seems to have originated around Naples, where the fishermen would cook their catch in seawater flavored with olive oil and vegetables. Today you find the Acqua Pazza preparation of fish in many coastal regions of Italy. It is always a soupy preparation, but can consist of anything from just a few simple vegetables in a broth to a thicker tomatoey broth, based on where you are. The fish is usually a firm white fish, such as grouper, but halibut or any fish in the bass family would work well in this preparation. I have somewhat modified and added my touch to this classic dish by including ditalini pasta. It makes for a complete meal.

In a large Dutch oven, combine the fish bones and heads, the tomatoes, lemon, garlic, peperoncini, parsley, bay leaves, wine, and olive oil. Season with 1 teaspoon salt, and add 6 cups cold water. Bring it to a simmer, and cook until the liquid is reduced by half, about 30 minutes.

Strain the liquid and return it to the pot, discarding the solids. Add the capers, olives, and the white parts of the scallions, and return to a simmer. Add the pasta, and simmer just until it's very al dente. Add the grouper fillets, and simmer until they're just cooked, about 5 minutes. Stir in the green parts of the scallions, and season with salt if needed. Transfer the fish to soup plates, and ladle the cooking liquid over it. Serve right away.

Baked Fresh Sardines

Sardine al Forno

Serves 4

1 pound fresh sardines, cleaned

¾ cup fine dried bread crumbs

½ cup freshly grated Grana Padano

3 tablespoons chopped
fresh Italian parsley

2 teaspoons chopped
fresh thyme leaves

¼ cup extra-virgin olive oil,
plus more for brushing

Kosher salt

12 fresh bay leaves, plus a
few more if needed

4 garlic cloves, sliced

When I was growing up in Istria, sardines were abundant, and easily found at the market in the morning. Frying or prepared in saor—a typical Venetian dish in which deep-fried sardines are marinated with onions in a sweetened vinegar—were typical preparations, but I loved them best (and still do!) baked in the oven with lots of fresh bay leaves. They are good hot or at room temperature and can be an appetizer, a full meal with some salad, or a snack when you have family or friends coming over for a glass of wine. Good dry white wine is the best with this; try some from the Friuli region, which makes some of Italy's best whites.

Preheat the oven to 400 degrees.

Soak the sardines briefly in cold water. Drain them. Open up the sardines by running your thumb along the inside of the stomach cavity. Remove the entire skeleton, and scrape away any remaining small bones with a paring knife. Rinse again, and pat them dry. (You can also ask your fishmonger to do this for you if it seems intimidating.)

In a medium bowl, combine the bread crumbs, Grana Padano, parsley, and thyme. Drizzle with 3 tablespoons of the oil, and season with ½ teaspoon salt. Toss with a fork. Brush a 9-by-13-inch baking dish with olive oil. Make a bed of bay leaves on the bottom. (They should be close together, but don't have to be touching.) Scatter the garlic over the top. Sprinkle with about a third of the crumb mixture. Lay the sardines open, skin side down, over the top. Sprinkle with the remaining crumbs. Drizzle with the remaining 1 tablespoon olive oil.

Bake until the tops are crisp and golden brown and the sardines are cooked through, 20 to 30 minutes. Remove the bay leaves as you are serving.

Easter family meal with my brother Franco's family at my house, 2015: (from left to right) Estelle, Eric, Josh, Corrado, Tanya (at the sink), me, Grandma Erminia, Margaret, and Franco

MEAT AND POULTRY

When I was growing up, our primary source of meat was the *animali del cortile,* or barnyard animals—all the smaller animals that ran around the barnyard—chickens, ducks, rabbits, goats, lambs, and pigs. We did not have cows, so beef was not a big part of our menu. Meat was expensive, and we used it mainly to make soup and sauces, and to dress pasta, polenta, or rice. Grandma Erminia was not a big meat-eater, maybe because, during her childhood and World War II, food—especially meat—was scarce. But she loved chicken, and during our first years in America, as young immigrants, we ate plenty of chicken wings and legs.

———————————

Rabbit in Tomato Sauce with Peppers   153

Pork Chops with Mushrooms and Pickled Peperoncini   154

Sausages with Mixed Greens   156

Spicy Vinegar Ribs and Potatoes   157

Roast Boneless Leg of Lamb   159

Lamb Stew with Peas   160

Liver Venetian-Style   161

Goulash   162

Beef Rollatini   164

Cheesy Baked Chicken Wings   167

Chicken Scaloppine with Prosciutto and Peas   168

Lidia's Simple Roast Chicken   169

Chicken Rollatini with Fontina and Artichokes   172

Turkey Stuffed Peppers   173

Roast Pork Shoulder   174

Rabbit in Tomato Sauce with Peppers

Coniglio in Salsa di Pomodoro con Peperoni

Serves 4

One 4-pound rabbit

Kosher salt

¼ cup extra-virgin olive oil

All-purpose flour, for dredging

1 large onion, thickly sliced

1 small red bell pepper, seeded, thickly sliced

1 small yellow bell pepper, seeded, thickly sliced

2 teaspoons chopped fresh rosemary

Peperoncino flakes

1 cup dry white wine

One 28-ounce can whole San Marzano tomatoes, crushed by hand

2 fresh bay leaves

¼ cup chopped fresh Italian parsley

I love rabbit—it is a flavorful and light meat, low in fat, and environmentally sustainable. My grandma Rosa kept a lot of animals in her courtyard: chickens, ducks, geese, pigeons, and rabbits. They made good, hearty sauces that Nonna Rosa used to dress pasta, polenta, or rice. Rabbits reproduce quickly and mature in four to five months. Though they require much feeding, they are happy with grass and leftover vegetable scraps. They love clover, and in the spring I used to go to a field and gather basketfuls for them. Rabbit can be a bit bony, so a good tip is to use rabbit legs. The hind legs are meatier and best. You could substitute six of the hind legs for the whole rabbit.

First, cut the rabbit into ten serving pieces (or ask your butcher to do it for you): Cut off the back legs, and cut at the joint to get 2 pieces per leg. Cut off the neck piece. Cut off the front legs, leaving them whole. Chop the saddle crosswise into three pieces. Season the rabbit all over with 1 teaspoon salt. Heat the oil in a large Dutch oven over medium-high heat. Spread a thin layer of flour on a plate. Lightly dredge the rabbit pieces in flour, and add them to the hot oil. Cook the pieces until they're browned on the underside, about 3 minutes; then turn them and brown the other side, about 3 minutes more. Remove them to a plate.

Add to the Dutch oven the onion and peppers, and season with 1 teaspoon salt. Cook and stir until the vegetables are slightly wilted, about 5 minutes. Add the rosemary and ¼ teaspoon peperoncino, and cook until they're sizzling, about 30 seconds; then add the white wine. Bring the liquid to a boil, and cook until it's reduced by half, about 2 minutes. Add the tomatoes, 1 cup water, and the bay leaves. Adjust the heat so the sauce is simmering, and nestle in the rabbit pieces. Cover, and simmer until the rabbit pieces are tender, about 30 to 40 minutes. Uncover, and bring to a rapid simmer to reduce the sauce slightly, if needed. Stir in the parsley, remove the bay leaves, and serve.

Pork Chops with Mushrooms and Pickled Peperoncini

Costolette di Maiale con Funghi e Peperoni Sottaceto

Serves 4

4 bone-in pork rib chops,
1 inch thick

Kosher salt

All-purpose flour, for dredging

3 tablespoons extra-virgin olive oil

8 pickled Tuscan peperoncini, plus
2 tablespoons brine from the jar

1 large red onion, cut into 8 wedges,
left attached at the root end

3 sprigs fresh thyme

1 pound mixed mushrooms
(such as cremini, shiitake, button),
thickly sliced or quartered

½ cup dry white wine

1 cup low-sodium chicken stock

¼ cup chopped fresh Italian
parsley

My family loves this dish. The pork is relatively low-fat for meat, and the pickled peperoncino peppers give the whole thing a bit of spicy kick. You can prepare this dish with rib pork chops, as called for in this recipe, or loin pork chops, which look like T-bones and are often less expensive. The one important thing to pay attention to is the size of the chops: make sure they are all about the same size, so they take the same time to cook. I really like pickled Tuscan peperoncini. I use them in an antipasto, in sandwiches, to make spicy pasta sauces, and I especially love to cook them with pork or chicken. They are a greenish-yellow color, about 1 to 1½ inches long, usually pickled whole with the stem on. You can find them in the Italian or Greek section of the grocery store, usually in a long cylindrical glass bottle.

Season the pork chops with ½ teaspoon salt. Spread some flour on a plate, and dredge the chops on both sides. Heat a large cast-iron skillet or low Dutch oven over medium-high heat. Add the olive oil. When the oil is hot, add the chops, and brown on one side, about 3 minutes. Flip, and brown the second side, 2 to 3 minutes more. Remove them to a plate.

Add the pickled peperoncini and brine. Let them sizzle for a minute; then add the red onion wedges and thyme sprigs and brown the onions on both cut sides, about 3 minutes. Add the mushrooms, and stir to coat them in the pan juices. Season with 1 teaspoon salt. Once the mushrooms have begun to wilt, add the white wine, and simmer to reduce it by half. Pour in the stock, and return the liquid to a simmer. Arrange the chops on top of the mushroom mixture, and cover. Adjust the heat to simmering, and simmer until the chops are just cooked through, about 10 minutes.

Uncover, and remove the chops to a platter or plates. Bring the sauce to a boil to reduce and thicken it slightly, about 1 minute. Stir the parsley into the sauce, then pour the sauce over the chops to serve.

Sausages with Mixed Greens

Salsicce con Verdure Miste

Serves 4 to 6

8 sweet Italian sausages
(about 2 pounds)

5 tablespoons extra-virgin olive oil

1 medium onion, sliced

4 garlic cloves, crushed and peeled

6 whole hot pickled cherry peppers,
plus ¼ cup brine from the jar

1 cup dry white wine

1 large bunch kale, stemmed,
coarsely chopped

1 teaspoon kosher salt

¼ teaspoon peperoncino flakes

1 large bunch mature spinach,
stemmed, coarsely chopped

Pickled hot cherry peppers are what make this dish, and some people in my family, mainly Corrado, my son-in-law, and my grandson Lorenzo, like it real hot . . . so they get a few extra peppers. These peppers bring spice, and their brine adds flavor and acidity. I use them often when cooking pork and chicken, and they are also delicious as part of an antipasto, or seeded and chopped in a sandwich, as well as in a tomato sauce for pasta. I always keep some in the refrigerator, where they keep for months. You can also find these little red peppers stuffed with tuna, which are delicious, and a particular favorite of my son, Joseph.

Prick the sausages all over with a fork. Heat 3 tablespoons of the olive oil in a large shallow braising pan or low Dutch oven over medium heat. Add the sausages, and cook until they're browned all over, about 8 minutes. Add the onion and garlic cloves, and cook until the onion wilts, 3 to 4 minutes. Add the peppers and their brine, as well as the white wine. Simmer to cook the sausages through, 8 to 10 minutes. Remove the sausages to a plate.

Add the remaining olive oil to the pan. Add the kale, and season with the salt and peperoncino flakes. Toss with tongs until the kale begins to wilt. Add ½ cup water, bring it to a simmer, and cover. Cook until the kale is almost tender, about 10 minutes.

Stir in the spinach, and simmer, uncovered, until the greens are both tender, 5 to 10 minutes more. Add the sausages on top, and simmer just to heat them through again, about 2 minutes.

Spicy Vinegar Ribs and Potatoes

Costolette di Maiale Piccanti all'Aceto con Patate

Serves 4 to 6

1 rack pork spare ribs
(about 2½ pounds),
cut into individual ribs

Kosher salt

3 tablespoons extra-virgin olive oil

6 garlic cloves, crushed and peeled

4 fresh bay leaves

4 sprigs fresh rosemary

1 cup low-sodium chicken stock

4 medium russet potatoes,
peel left on, cut into thick
wedges (about 2 pounds)

1 cup dry white wine

½ cup red wine vinegar

3 tablespoons honey

½ teaspoon ground cayenne

Everyone loves ribs, whether barbecued or served some other way—so try this Italian rendition. It's a great dish to make when you have a larger gathering; just multiply the recipe. Make sure you have one or more large roasting pans, because you want to allow space for the ribs and the potatoes to brown and get crispy. These are something we really get into as a family, because they are finger-licking good, and a lot of finger licking definitely happens when I serve this dish.

Preheat the oven to 425 degrees.

Pat the ribs very dry with paper towels, and season them with 1 teaspoon salt. Put the ribs in a large heavy-duty roasting pan. Drizzle with the olive oil, and add the garlic, bay leaves, and rosemary. Pour in the stock, and toss to combine everything. Roast, stirring once halfway through, until the ribs are browned and the stock is evaporated, about 45 minutes.

Add the potatoes, and toss them well. Continue to roast until the potatoes begin to take on a little color, 10 to 15 minutes. Meanwhile, combine the wine, vinegar, honey, and cayenne in a spouted measuring cup. Drizzle this over the potatoes and ribs, and stir well.

Move the pan to the lowest part of the oven. Continue roasting, stirring every 5 minutes or so, until the ribs and potatoes are tender and nicely glazed, about 20 minutes more. Tip the pan, spoon out excess fat, and discard the rosemary and bay leaves. Serve hot.

Roast Boneless Leg of Lamb

Cosciotto d'Agnello Arrosto Disossato

Serves 8

1 cup fresh Italian parsley leaves

8 garlic cloves, crushed and peeled

3 tablespoons fresh rosemary leaves

¼ cup plus 2 tablespoons
extra-virgin olive oil

3 tablespoons Dijon mustard

Kosher salt

Peperoncino flakes

5-pound boneless leg of lamb

3 large carrots,
cut into 2-inch chunks

3 large parsnips,
cut into 2-inch chunks

8 cipollini onions, peeled
but left whole

2 cups dry white wine

2 cups low-sodium chicken stock

For lamb lovers, rack of lamb can be expensive, so roasting a boneless leg of lamb is a good option. You might find it tied, ready to roast; if not, the butcher can debone it for you. If it is tied, I untie it and season it with a paste of herbs and mustard. I make this paste with lots of garlic, rosemary, and mustard, spread it on the open leg of lamb, then tie it tight and spread the paste on the outside as well. I set the lamb on a bed of cipollini onions, parsnips, and carrots, to impart their flavor to the lamb as it roasts. In the end, you serve flavorful slices of the roasted lamb on top of mixed roasted vegetables. It makes a big impression at celebratory events, especially when you present the whole roast leg of lamb to your crowd of guests.

Preheat the oven to 400 degrees.

Combine the parsley, garlic, rosemary, ¼ cup of the olive oil, the mustard, 1 teaspoon salt, and a big pinch of peperoncino in a mini–food processor. Pulse to make a paste.

Open the lamb up on the cutting board. Spread with half of the herb-and-garlic paste. Roll up the lamb, and tie with kitchen twine in four places, crosswise, to close the leg into a roll. Thread one piece of string through the others lengthwise, and tie to close the ends. Spread the rest of the paste over the outside of the lamb.

Scatter the carrots, parsnips, and onions in the bottom of a large roasting pan that can also go on the stovetop, and drizzle everything with the remaining 2 tablespoons olive oil. Toss well, and season with 1 teaspoon salt. Set the lamb on top, and pour the wine and stock into the pan.

Roast until the lamb reads 130 degrees in the center for medium, about 1½ hours. Remove to a cutting board to rest for 15 minutes.

Meanwhile, set the roasting pan with the vegetables in it over medium heat. Bring the pan juices to a simmer, and cook until they're slightly reduced, 2 to 3 minutes. Cut the strings from the lamb, and slice the lamb against the grain. Serve with the sauce and vegetables on the side.

Lamb Stew with Peas

Spezzatino d'Agnello con Piselli

Serves 4 to 6

6 cups low-sodium chicken stock

1 teaspoon saffron threads

3 pounds bone-in lamb shoulder chops, about 1 inch thick, cut into 3-inch pieces

Kosher salt

All-purpose flour, for dredging

3 tablespoons extra-virgin olive oil

1 medium onion, chopped

3 garlic cloves, crushed and peeled

3 tablespoons tomato paste

½ teaspoon peperoncino flakes

1½ cups dry white wine

2 fresh bay leaves

16 ounces frozen peas

¼ cup chopped fresh Italian parsley

"Spezzatino" means "pieces of meat." In Italy, spezzatinos are made from a variety of meats: *manzo* (beef), *vitello* (veal), *maiale* (pork), and, of course, *agnello* (lamb). A spezzatino is usually made from secondary cuts, generally muscle from the leg or shoulder. Because these are tougher cuts, it does take longer to cook, which gives you more time to add additional flavorings, plus some vegetables to make a complete meal. Braising is a good cooking technique, especially in the fall and winter, but when I make this lamb rendition, I like to make it in the spring and use shelled fresh peas. My grandmother would send me to the garden to harvest the mature pea pods, the large and full ones, and then I would have to shell them for her. Every now and then, I would pop some peas into my mouth. My family loves long-cooked stews and braised meats, and Corrado, my Roman son-in-law, particularly loves them made with lamb.

Bring the stock to a simmer in a small saucepan. Add the saffron, remove the pan from the heat, and let it steep while you brown the lamb.

Season the lamb with 1 teaspoon salt. Spread some flour on a plate. Dredge the lamb pieces in the flour. Heat a large shallow Dutch oven over medium-high heat, and add the olive oil. When the oil is hot, add the chops, and brown them on both sides, about 8 minutes in all. Remove them to a plate.

Reduce the heat to medium, and add the onion and garlic cloves. Cook and stir until they begin to soften, about 4 minutes. Make a space in the pan, and add the tomato paste to that spot. Cook and stir the tomato paste there for a minute, until it darkens a shade or two; then add a large pinch of peperoncino. Stir the tomato paste into the onion mixture, and then add the white wine. Bring it to a simmer, and simmer until the liquid is reduced by about half, 2 to 3 minutes. Pour in 3 cups of the chicken stock with the saffron, and add the bay leaves. Bring it to a simmer, and cook, uncovered, until the lamb chops are almost tender, about 1 hour and 15 minutes, adding the remaining stock in several additions when the pan begins to dry out.

Add the peas, and simmer until they're tender, 8 to 10 minutes more. Remove the bay leaves, sprinkle with the parsley, stir, and serve.

Liver Venetian-Style

Fegato alla Veneziana

Serves 4 to 6

¼ cup extra-virgin olive oil

2 large white onions, thinly sliced

1 pound mixed mushrooms (button, cremini, oyster, shiitake, chanterelle, etc.), thickly sliced

6 fresh bay leaves

Kosher salt

¼ cup red wine vinegar

¼ cup dry white wine

2 tablespoons unsalted butter

Vegetable oil, for frying the liver

1½ pounds calf's liver, sliced ½ inch thick, cut into 3-inch pieces

Freshly ground black pepper

All-purpose flour, for dredging

¼ cup chopped fresh Italian parsley

If you like liver as much as I do (I enjoy it at least once a month), you'll love this. Liver veneziana—liver Venetian-style—the way my mother made it, is particularly delicious, with everything cooked together in one pan. Liver is sensitive to temperature and gets overcooked easily, so in this version, I sauté the traditional onions and some mushrooms with the vinegar and wine and all the Venetian flavors. Then I sear the liver separately, forming a crust and leaving the inside tender. I combine the two, mixing just to combine the flavors, and serve. This was a favorite of my father and my mother, so we ate it often. My father loved it served with polenta, and I still prefer it that way. I sometimes prepare chicken livers the same way; just make sure you remove all the ligaments and fat, and cook the liver lobes whole.

Heat a large skillet over medium-low heat. Add the olive oil. When the oil is hot, add the onions. Cook and stir until soft but without color, about 10 minutes. Add the mushrooms, bay leaves, and 1 teaspoon salt, and stir to combine. Cover, and cook until the mushrooms give up their juices, about 5 minutes. Uncover, increase the heat to medium high, and cook until the juices have reduced away and the mushrooms are wilted, 3 to 4 minutes.

Add the vinegar and wine and bring to a simmer. Cook until the liquid is slightly thickened, 1 to 2 minutes. Remove the bay leaves and whisk in the butter. Keep this mixture warm while you cook the liver.

Heat a thin film of vegetable oil in a large nonstick skillet over medium-high heat. Season the liver with 1½ teaspoons salt and several grinds of pepper. Spread some flour on a plate. Lightly dredge the liver in the flour, and add it to the hot oil. Cook until the pieces are nicely browned but not totally cooked through, about 1 minute per side. Remove them to a platter. Top with the onion mixture, and sprinkle with the parsley. Serve immediately.

Goulash

Serves 6 to 8

3 pounds boneless beef chuck,
cut into 2-inch chunks

Kosher salt

All-purpose flour, for dredging

¼ cup extra-virgin olive oil

3 garlic cloves, crushed and peeled

2 medium onions, chopped

1½ cups dry white wine

5 tablespoons tomato paste

5 fresh bay leaves

2 tablespoons sweet paprika

Grated zest of 1 lemon

6 cups low-sodium chicken stock

3 medium carrots,
cut into 2-inch chunks

3 medium russet potatoes,
cut into 2-inch chunks

"Goulash" is not an Italian word and not an Italian preparation, but it is common in Istria, where I was born. That part of Italy, in what is now Croatia, was under the rule of so many empires, governments, and cultures, from Roman, Byzantine, Frankish, Venetian, Hapsburg, Napoleonic, Austrian, Italian, and Yugoslavian, to Croatian. Goulash, the national dish of Hungary, came with one of those occupations, and it remained. It is a preparation that, with the addition of potatoes, makes a whole and filling meal. Since it uses a secondary cut of meat, it's economical as well. Paprika is the seasoning that identifies Hungarian cooking. It comes in sweet, spicy, and even smoked forms, usually milled into a powder. Here I use sweet paprika, but feel free to spice or smoke it up if you like.

Season the beef with 1 teaspoon salt. Spread the flour on a plate. Heat a large Dutch oven over medium heat, and add the olive oil. When the oil is hot, dredge the beef in flour, add about half of the beef to the pot, and brown it on all sides, removing the pieces to a plate as they brown and adding more.

When all of the beef is out of the pot, add the garlic and onions. Stir to coat the onions in the oil. Add ½ cup of the white wine, and simmer until the onions have softened, about 5 minutes. Adjust the heat to reduce away the wine, about 1 minute. Make a space in the pan, and add the tomato paste to that spot. Cook and stir the tomato paste there for a minute, until it darkens a shade or two; then stir it into the onions. Add the bay leaves, paprika, and lemon zest, and stir to combine.

Add the remaining 1 cup wine, and bring it to a simmer, stirring to loosen any browned bits from the bottom of the pot. Add 3 cups of the stock, and bring it to a simmer. Add the beef and carrots and 2 teaspoons salt. Cover, and simmer until the beef is nearly tender, about 1 hour.

Uncover, stir in the potatoes, and add enough of the remaining stock to cover them. Simmer, uncovered, adding more stock as needed to keep everything covered, until the beef and potatoes are very tender, 45 minutes to 1 hour more. Remove the bay leaves, and serve.

Beef Rollatini

Rollatini di Manzo

Serves 8

FOR THE BEEF

3 pounds boneless beef eye of round

3 cups cubed crustless day-old country bread

1 cup grated provola

½ cup freshly grated Grana Padano

½ cup chopped fresh Italian parsley

4 scallions, chopped

4 ounces prosciutto cotto, thickly sliced, diced

1 teaspoon garlic powder

Kosher salt

FOR THE SAUCE

¼ cup extra-virgin olive oil

All-purpose flour, for dredging

1 large onion, chopped

1 cup dry red wine

Kosher salt

Two 28-ounce cans whole San Marzano tomatoes, crushed by hand

3 fresh bay leaves

1 teaspoon dried oregano, preferably Sicilian oregano on the branch

¼ teaspoon peperoncino flakes

Beef rollatini was not a dish I often ate growing up. Beef was scarce, and this was not a style of cooking my grandma often used, but I learned to make it as a young woman in America, as I became familiar with Italian American restaurant food here. Bracciole, as this dish is also called, were commonly cooked in Sunday sauce, a tomato-based sauce with meat, along with sausages, ribs, and meatballs, and were served as a second course, after the pasta dressed with the sauce. If you double the recipe, a big pot of these goes a long way in serving a tableful of hungry guests. Use a large piece of eye of round to get nice, even-sized slices of beef. You'll have extra sauce here, which will be very flavorful from the long cooking of the beef rolls. You can use it to dress a separate pasta course for the same meal, or to save for another day.

For the beef: Use a sharp knife to slice the beef into eight slices against the grain. Pound them with a meat mallet to make all of the slices an even thickness, just shy of ½ inch thick.

Put the bread in a bowl, and add water to cover. Let it soak until it's moistened; then squeeze the water out of the bread and discard all of the water. Put the bread back in the bowl, along with the provola, Grana Padano, parsley, scallions, prosciutto cotto, garlic powder, and ½ teaspoon salt. Mix well to form a cohesive stuffing.

Lay the beef slices out on your work surface with the long sides facing you. Season them with salt, flip them, and season the other sides. Divide the filling among the slices, leaving about an inch border all around. Roll them up, tuck the ends in, and seal with toothpicks to keep the rolls from unrolling. Season the outside of the rolls with salt.

For the sauce: Heat the olive oil in a large Dutch oven over medium heat. Spread some flour on a plate. When the oil is hot, lightly dredge the rolls in flour, and brown them on all sides, in batches, about 5 minutes per batch. Remove them to a plate as they brown.

Once all of the rolls are out, add the onion. Cook, stirring occasionally, until it's wilted, 4 to 5 minutes. Add the wine and 1 teaspoon salt. Bring the liquid to a simmer, stirring with a wooden spoon to loosen the browned bits from the bottom of the pan. Reduce the wine by half, about 2 minutes; then add the tomatoes and 3 cups water. Add the bay leaves, oregano, 2 teaspoons salt, and the peperoncino. Bring the sauce to a simmer, and nestle the rolls in the sauce. Simmer, covered, until the beef is almost tender, about 1 hour. Uncover, and continue to simmer until the rolls are very tender but not falling apart and the sauce is thick and flavorful, about 30 minutes more. Remove the rolls to a platter and remove the toothpicks. Remove the bay leaves, and serve the rolls with the sauce.

Cheesy Baked Chicken Wings

Alette di Pollo al Formaggio al Forno

Serves 4

2 pounds chicken wing segments

Kosher salt

4 tablespoons unsalted butter, melted, cooled slightly

½ cup fine dried bread crumbs

½ cup freshly grated Grana Padano

1 teaspoon dried oregano, preferably Sicilian oregano on the branch

½ teaspoon garlic powder

Marinara (page 7), warmed, for dipping

Chicken wings are always welcome in my house, especially if I have a large family gathering, and I bet they're a favorite in yours as well. Usually, they are fried, but here you have a recipe for an oven-baked version that is just as crispy and delicious. The grandkids love them, and I usually need to make a few baking-tray-fulls of them. You can also use this recipe to bread and bake vegetables, shrimp, scallops, and more. The baking time might vary, and tough vegetables, like carrots or cauliflower, might need to be blanched lightly before breading.

Preheat the oven to 425 degrees. Line a baking sheet with parchment.

Put the wings in a large bowl, and season them with 1 teaspoon salt. Drizzle them with the melted butter, and toss to coat them evenly.

In another large bowl, combine the bread crumbs, Grana Padano, oregano, garlic powder, and ½ teaspoon salt. Add half of the wings, and toss to coat them well in the crumbs. Arrange them on the baking sheet, making sure the wings don't touch. Repeat with the remaining wings. If there are any crumbs left in the bowl, sprinkle them on top of the wings. Roast until the wings are crispy, golden, and tender, 35 to 40 minutes. Serve with warm marinara for dipping.

Chicken Scaloppine with Prosciutto and Peas

Scaloppine di Pollo con Prosciutto e Piselli

Serves 4

4 small boneless, skinless chicken breasts (about 6 ounces each)

Kosher salt and freshly ground black pepper

8 large fresh sage leaves

4 slices prosciutto

All-purpose flour, for dredging

2 tablespoons extra-virgin olive oil

4 tablespoons unsalted butter

2 shallots, finely chopped

1 cup dry white wine

1 cup low-sodium chicken stock

1 cup frozen peas

¼ cup chopped fresh Italian parsley

Prosciutto and peas seem to be a match made in heaven. In our family, we often make just prosciutto and peas in olive oil with some sautéed chopped onion, as a vegetable or a pasta dressing. The chicken here rounds it out to an easy and full meal for the family. Chicken is the most popular meat in the United States, and chicken breasts seem to be the favorite part, but we all know that they can become dry and tough if not cooked properly. This recipe is tasty and easy to make, and keeps your chicken moist. You can also add mushrooms to this preparation; cook them with the shallots, and then proceed with the dish.

With a sharp knife, butterfly the chicken breasts open by slicing crosswise almost all the way through and opening up each breast like a book. Pound them gently, just to even the pieces out to about ½ inch thick overall.

Season the scaloppine with salt and pepper, and press 2 sage leaves into the center of each. Top each with a slice of prosciutto, and wrap the edges around the chicken. Tap with the back of a chef's knife to adhere the prosciutto to the chicken.

Spread the flour on a plate. Heat a large skillet over medium-low heat, and add the olive oil. When the oil is hot, add 2 tablespoons of the butter and let it melt. Lightly dredge the scaloppine in flour and add them to the skillet, prosciutto side down, as many at a time as will fit without touching each other. Cook to brown the prosciutto gently, 2 to 3 minutes per side. Remove them to a paper-towel-lined plate as they brown, and cook the rest the same way.

Once all of the scaloppine are out of the skillet, add the shallots and remaining 2 tablespoons butter. Cook until the shallots are softened, about 4 minutes. Pour in the white wine, bring it to a boil, and reduce it by half, about 2 minutes. Add the chicken stock, bring the liquid to a simmer, and add the scaloppine and peas. Simmer until the sauce is slightly thickened and the peas are tender, 4 to 5 minutes. Stir in the parsley, and serve.

Lidia's Simple Roast Chicken

Pollo Arrosto alla Lidia

Serves 4

4 sprigs fresh rosemary

2 lemons, zested and quartered lengthwise

1 teaspoon garlic powder

Large (4-to-5-pound) roasting chicken

Kosher salt and freshly ground black pepper

¼ cup extra-virgin olive oil

1 pound large carrots, cut into 2-inch chunks

1 pound small red potatoes (halved if larger than walnuts)

1 cup dry white wine

½ cup low-sodium chicken stock

Every chef has a favorite rendition of roast chicken. In mine, rosemary and lemon are the main flavors. I stuff the lemon, rosemary, and garlic under the skin and in the cavity, and I add some vegetables to roast around the chicken so they absorb the flavors as well. Served with a salad, this makes a complete meal. It was a favorite dish for me and my mother to share when it was just the two of us at home. Her favorite part was the wings, which she would eat with great care, down to every last morsel. What we had left over, we would turn into salad for lunch the next day, and then we'd make soup with the carcass. Chicken was Grandma's favorite meat, whether in a soup, roasted, breaded, or in sauce to dress pasta. So I cooked chicken a lot for the two of us, especially as she got on in years. It made me so happy to see how she still enjoyed eating, well into her hundredth year, but let me tell you, she would let me know if the flavors were not right on target.

Preheat the oven to 400 degrees.

Remove the leaves from 2 sprigs rosemary, and chop them. Add them to a small bowl with the lemon zest and garlic powder, and mix to combine. Loosen the skin on the chicken breast, and spread half of the mixture under it, taking care not to break the skin. Spread the rest over the chicken, and season all over and inside the cavity with 2 teaspoons salt and pepper to taste. Rub the chicken all over with 2 tablespoons of the olive oil. Stuff the lemon quarters and remaining rosemary sprigs in the cavity. Cut a small slit to loosen the skin on both sides of the breast cavity, and stick the opposite leg in each side, an easy way to truss it. Tuck the wings under the bottom of the bird.

Put the carrots and potatoes in a metal roasting pan large enough to fit the chicken without crowding, and season them with 1 teaspoon salt. Toss with the remaining 2 tablespoons of the olive oil. Pour in the white wine and stock, and set the chicken on the bed of vegetables.

Roast, basting halfway through, until the chicken is golden brown and the internal temperature in the deepest part of the thigh reads 165 degrees, →

← 1 hour and 15 minutes to 1½ hours. Set the chicken on a cutting board to rest for 15 minutes.

While the chicken is resting, set the roasting pan over medium-high heat and bring the pan juices to a boil, to glaze the carrots and potatoes. Carve the chicken, and serve with the carrots and potatoes, spooning the pan juices over.

Chicken Rollatini with Fontina and Artichokes

Rollatini di Pollo con Fontina e Carciofi

Serves 4

3 ripe plum tomatoes, diced

½ small red onion, chopped

One 14-ounce can quartered artichoke hearts, drained, chopped

2 tablespoons extra-virgin olive oil

2 tablespoons red wine vinegar

Kosher salt

4 medium boneless, skinless chicken breasts (about 8 ounces each)

1 cup grated Italian Fontina

½ cup freshly grated Grana Padano

2 tablespoons chopped fresh Italian parsley

All-purpose flour, for dredging

2 large eggs

1½ cups fine dried bread crumbs

Vegetable oil, for frying

½ cup fresh basil leaves, chopped

I am often asked, "My family loves chicken; how can I make it differently tonight?" Well, this is a little more complex recipe for chicken, full of surprises and flavor. It has a crunchy crust with a melted cheese stuffing, and can be made in advance and reheated in the oven just before serving. Top it with a salad of fresh tomato, basil, and onion, and it makes a complete meal. I love the artichokes in the filling, but you could also use chopped cooked spinach or roll in some asparagus spears.

For the topping: Combine the tomatoes, red onion, half of the artichoke hearts, the olive oil, vinegar, and 1 teaspoon salt in a medium bowl. Toss well, and set aside to let the flavors develop while you make the chicken.

With a sharp knife, butterfly the chicken breasts open by slicing crosswise almost all the way through and opening up each breast like a book. Pound gently, just to even the pieces out to about ½ inch thick. Season on both sides with salt.

Combine the Fontina, remaining artichokes, Grana Padano, and parsley in a small bowl, and toss to make a cohesive stuffing. Spread the stuffing on the chicken breasts, leaving a border around the edges. Roll them up, starting with the short sides, to enclose the stuffing. (The chicken roll should stay closed; you can use toothpicks if you like, but be sure to remove them when you serve.)

Spread the flour in a shallow bowl. Beat the eggs in a second shallow bowl with 2 tablespoons water, and spread the bread crumbs in a third.

Heat 1 inch of vegetable oil in a large skillet over medium heat until a few bread crumbs sizzle on contact. Dredge the rollatini in flour, then eggs, then bread crumbs, coating them completely.

Carefully add the rollatini to the oil, and cook, turning occasionally, until they're crisped and browned all over and the chicken is cooked through, 8 to 10 minutes. Remove them to a paper-towel-lined plate. Season them lightly with salt, and slice them into thick rounds. Stir the basil into the tomato topping, and serve it with the rollatini.

Turkey Stuffed Peppers

Peperoni Ripieni di Tacchino

Serves 6

3 tablespoons extra-virgin olive oil

1 large onion, finely chopped

3 cups tomato passata

1 teaspoon dried oregano, preferably Sicilian oregano on the branch

Kosher salt

3 fresh bay leaves

4 cups day-old bread cubes (from a sturdy loaf)

1 medium carrot, shredded

1 medium zucchini, shredded

1 cup freshly grated Grana Padano

¼ cup chopped fresh Italian parsley

2 large eggs, beaten

Freshly ground black pepper

1½ pounds ground turkey (93/7)

6 medium red, yellow, or orange bell peppers

We always made stuffed peppers when I was a child, and even though this dish seems to have Eastern European roots, it is a tradition in our house, especially when the peppers are abundant. The chopped meat for the stuffing was a blend of pork, beef, and veal. Here the dish is a little lighter, using ground turkey and some vegetables as well. It is easy and foolproof. Be careful not to overstuff the peppers: the stuffing will expand out of the peppers if you do. This dish keeps well in the refrigerator, and when my mother was alive, I would freeze them in pint containers with some sauce and label them so she would have a meal ready if I was traveling or getting home late.

Heat a large Dutch oven (large enough to hold the peppers) over medium heat. Add the olive oil. When the oil is hot, add the onion, and cook until it's tender, about 8 minutes. Add the passata, and rinse out the bottle with 2 cups water, adding the water to the pot. Then add the oregano, 1 teaspoon salt, and the bay leaves. Bring to a simmer, and let cook while you stuff the peppers.

Put the bread cubes in a bowl, and add warm water to cover. Let them soak until they're just softened, about 5 minutes. Squeeze out the excess water, and place the bread in a large bowl. Put the carrot and zucchini in a dish towel, and wring out any excess moisture. Add them to the bowl, along with the grated cheese, parsley, and eggs. Season the mixture with 1 teaspoon salt and several grinds of black pepper. Crumble in the turkey, and mix all to combine.

Cut the tops from the peppers, and remove the seeds and ribs. Divide the stuffing among the peppers. (If you have any leftover stuffing, depending on the size of your peppers, make the remainder into a few meatballs, and bake them on a sheet pan at 350 degrees for 15 minutes to set them, then cook them alongside the peppers in the sauce.) Nestle the peppers in the sauce, adjust the heat so the sauce is simmering around them, and cover. Cook until the peppers are tender and the filling is cooked through, 45 minutes to 1 hour. Pluck out the bay leaves and serve.

Roast Pork Shoulder

Spalla di Maiale Arrosto con Sidro di Mele, Sedano e Cipolle

Serves 8 or more

FOR THE SEASONING PASTE

1 medium onion, cut into chunks

1 stalk celery, cut into chunks

10 garlic cloves, crushed and peeled

Leaves from 3 sprigs fresh rosemary (about 2 tablespoons)

Leaves from 6 sprigs fresh thyme (about 2 tablespoons)

2 tablespoons porcini powder

Kosher salt

3 tablespoons extra-virgin olive oil

FOR THE PORK, VEGETABLES, AND SAUCE

1 bone-in pork shoulder roast (about 6 pounds)

Kosher salt

2 tablespoons extra-virgin olive oil

3 medium carrots, cut into large chunks

4 stalks celery, cut into large chunks

3 medium onions, cut into large chunks

4 garlic cloves, crushed and peeled

3 cups low-sodium chicken stock

2 cups apple cider

½ cup brandy

You probably know dried porcini mushrooms, but porcini powder is something you might not be too familiar with. I use a lot of dried porcini in my cooking, for rubs, marinades, and stuffings; for me it is the Italian umami. You can purchase ground porcini powder, or make your own by grinding dried porcini in a spice grinder. I foraged for porcini as a young girl, and also in Long Island and upstate New York. Porcini are best eaten fresh, but if you happen to have a huge find of porcini, it is good to dry those you can't eat right away and make your own porcini powder. Roast pork shoulder is another one of those festive preparations that require time to cook, but the oven does most of the work, and yields delicious results in abundance.

For the seasoning paste: Combine the onion, celery, garlic, rosemary, thyme, porcini powder, and 1 teaspoon salt in a food processor. Process to make a paste. With the processor running, add the olive oil, and process until it's incorporated.

To prepare the pork: Season the roast all over with 1 tablespoon salt. Rub it with 2 tablespoons of olive oil. With a sharp knife, cut deep slits all over the flesh of the roast, spacing them 2 or 3 inches apart. Fill the slits with some of the paste, and rub the rest all over the roast. Set the roast, fat/skin side up, on a rack in a large heavy-duty roasting pan. Let it sit at room temperature for 1 hour.

Preheat the oven to 425 degrees. Once the roast has rested, roast it for 1 hour. Reduce the oven temperature to 350 degrees. Remove the roasting pan from the oven, and remove the roast and rack. To the roasting pan, add the carrots, celery, onions, garlic, 2 cups of the chicken stock, the apple cider, brandy, and 1 teaspoon salt. Place the roast back in the pan, on top of the vegetables. Roast until the pork reaches an internal temperature of 175 degrees on an instant-read thermometer, 3½ to 4½ hours, depending on size, and then remove it from the pan.

Mash everything in the roasting pan, then pour it through a strainer into a large saucepan. Press on the solids with a wooden spoon to pass them through the strainer. Discard anything that remains in the strainer. Defat the juices by skimming the fat from the top with a spoon or using a fat-separator measuring cup. Bring the defatted juices to a simmer. Add the remaining cup of chicken stock, and boil to reduce the sauce and thicken it slightly, 4 to 5 minutes.

To serve, cut the meat from the bone and slice it. Arrange the slices on a platter, and serve the sauce alongside.

Grandma Erminia, with the other salesgirls, in Walken's Bake Shop in
Astoria, Queens, 1974: (from left to right) Nada, Josie, and Erminia

DESSERTS

If there is one chapter in this book that would make Grandma Erminia smile, it is this one, the dessert chapter. She loved sweets. Yes, candy and chocolate, but it was cakes that she enjoyed the most. When I was a child, even sugar for morning coffee was scarce and expensive, so I'm sure she was making up for what she had missed out on. Once we were in America as immigrants, I got a part-time job on weekends at Walken's Bake Shop just across from us on Broadway and Thirtieth Street in Astoria, Queens. After a few months, they needed more help and asked if I knew of anyone. They hired my mother as a full-time salesgirl! Astoria was a very ethnic community, with many Italians, and her broken English was accepted. She worked there for more than twenty years. I need not tell you that in those years she had her fill of desserts. She said that that was the sweetest time in her life. She would bring home all the imperfect and broken desserts, and the party would continue, for the family and the neighbors.

St. Joseph's Zeppole   180

Strawberry and Cream Parfaits   183

"Cat Tongue" Cookies   184

Apricot Jam Half-Moons   185

Rum Raisin Semifreddo   186

Kaiserschmarrn   188

Chocolate Ricotta Brick Cake   190

Chocolate Cherry Panettone   191

Chocolate Amaretti   195

Roasted Cranberries and Pears over Ice Cream   196

Mimosa Cake   197

In my kitchen, making Christmas cookies, 2005: (from left to right)
Julia, Ethan, Grandma Erminia, Lorenzo, me, Miles, and Olivia

St. Joseph's Zeppole

Zeppole di San Giuseppe

Makes about 18

FOR THE PASTRY CREAM

1½ cups whole milk

1 vanilla bean, split

4 large egg yolks

½ cup granulated sugar

⅓ cup cornstarch

2 tablespoons unsalted butter, cut into pieces

FOR THE ZEPPOLE

Vegetable oil, for frying

6 tablespoons unsalted butter, cut into pieces

1 tablespoon granulated sugar

½ teaspoon salt

1 cup all-purpose flour

4 large eggs

1 teaspoon grated lemon zest

Amarena cherries, for topping

Confectioners' sugar, for dusting

Zeppole di San Giuseppe are usually made to honor St. Joseph on his feast day of March 19, which is when Father's Day is celebrated in Italy. "Zeppole" can refer to many different desserts in Italy, such as fried dough with pine nuts and raisins, or fried dough with powdered sugar. It is the filling and presentation that make this recipe special and different.

You can find St. Joseph's zeppole all over Italy on March 19. It is amazing to see how food is integral to celebrations and holidays all over the world. But in Italy, a holiday is not a holiday without its designated food, and desserts are especially prominent. Give me a dessert and I will tell you which holiday it is connected to.

For the pastry cream: Put the milk in a medium saucepan, scrape the seeds from the vanilla bean in, and add the pod. Heat this over low heat until it's steaming, and let it steep for 5 minutes.

Whisk the egg yolks, sugar, and cornstarch in a large bowl. While still whisking, slowly pour in the milk mixture. Pour the mixture back into the saucepan, and set it over medium-low heat. Cook, whisking constantly, until a few bubbles pop to the surface and the mixture has thickened, 3 to 4 minutes. Remove the pan from the heat, and whisk in the butter a few pieces at a time until the mixture is smooth. Remove the vanilla bean. Strain the pastry cream into a clean bowl, press plastic wrap on its surface, and refrigerate until it's chilled, at least 4 hours.

For the zeppole: Pour 2 inches of oil into a Dutch oven, and heat it to 350 degrees.

Combine 1 cup water, the butter, sugar, and salt in a medium saucepan, and bring the liquid to a boil over medium heat. Once the butter melts and the mixture is at a full boil, add the flour all at once. Stir vigorously with a wooden spoon until the dough forms a smooth ball and comes away from the sides of the pan, leaving a thin film, 1 to 2 minutes.

Remove the pan from the heat. This next part can be done by hand with some elbow grease, or in a stand mixer: Let the dough cool for a minute, so the eggs don't scramble; then begin to beat the eggs in one at a time, fully incorporating each one before adding the next. Once all of the eggs are added, beat the dough until the it's thick, smooth, and glossy. Beat in the lemon zest.

Drop heaping tablespoons of dough into the hot oil, and cook, turning occasionally, until they're puffed and deep golden brown, about 6 to 7 minutes. (Fry in 2 batches, if needed; don't crowd the pan.)

Once the puffs have cooled, split them in half crosswise and lay the bottoms, cut side up, on a serving platter. Fill a pastry bag fitted with a large star tip with the custard. Pipe custard onto the bottoms (reserving a little for the top). Lay the reserved puff halves on top. Pipe a small star on top of each with the remaining custard. Top each with an Amarena cherry. Dust with confectioners' sugar on the platter, and serve.

Strawberry and Cream Parfaits

Parfait di Fragola e Crema

Makes 6 parfaits

1 pint ripe strawberries, sliced, plus 6 small whole strawberries for garnish

¼ cup fragola or other strawberry liqueur

¼ cup plus 2 tablespoons confectioners' sugar

3 tablespoons strawberry jam

1 cup heavy cream, chilled

1 pound mascarpone

1 teaspoon pure vanilla extract

3 cups coarsely crumbled crisp Italian cookies, such as "Cat Tongue" Cookies (recipe follows) or savoiardi

As a teenage immigrant in America, I discovered strawberries and cream, which instantly became one of my favorite desserts. I love the sweetness of locally grown strawberries with cream, a combination that tastes fresh and not too sweet. You can also layer this in an 8-by-8-inch baking pan for a more tiramisù-like dessert. Use any crisp, plain cookie you like for the crumbles here, or make my "Cat Tongue" Cookies (recipe follows). Early in my days in America, on weekends I worked in Walken's Bake Shop in Astoria, owned by the family of Christopher Walken, who is still a friend to this day. His father, who was of German descent, was a wonderful baker. The bakery had a great selection of delicious breads, cookies, and cakes; strawberry shortcake was one of their biggest sellers. On Sunday, after church, such a long line formed that they could not make the strawberry shortcakes fast enough. I loved them then, and I love this variation now.

Combine the sliced strawberries, fragola, and ¼ cup confectioners' sugar in a medium bowl, and let the strawberries rest for 30 minutes to release their juices. After 30 minutes, add the jam, and toss to combine well.

Meanwhile, in a stand mixer fitted with the whisk attachment, beat the cream and remaining 2 tablespoons confectioners' sugar to soft peaks. Put the mascarpone in a medium bowl, whisk by hand to lighten it, and then fold it into the whipped cream. Stir in the vanilla.

To assemble: Cover the bottom of six parfait glasses with some of the crumbled cookies or savoiardi. Top with half of the strawberry mixture. Top with half of the cream mixture, then a little more than half of the remaining cookies. Add the remaining strawberries, then cream. Refrigerate until the parfaits are chilled, at least 2 hours. To serve: Top with the remaining crumbled cookies and a strawberry.

"Cat Tongue" Cookies

Lingue di Gatto

Makes about 2 dozen

1 stick unsalted butter,
at room temperature

¾ cup confectioners' sugar

3 large egg whites,
at room temperature

1 teaspoon pure vanilla extract

1 teaspoon freshly grated
lemon zest

¾ cup all-purpose flour

Pinch of kosher salt

The Italian name of this easy-to-make cookie translates to "cats' tongues" because of their shape when baked. They are crispy and crunchy, almost a bit abrasive, also like the tongue of a cat. They're a great basic cookie to have in the house so you can assemble a quick dessert, or just to dunk in an espresso. I often made a few trays of these cookies and put them in a cookie tin for my mother to eat whenever she had a hankering for something sweet; she loved her sweets. I also always had a tin of chocolates on hand, and after a meal she would pull out her tins and choose one of each—never too many, just enough to have a little something sweet after her meal.

Preheat the oven to 375 degrees. Line two baking sheets with parchment or silicone baking mats.

Beat the butter in a stand mixer fitted with the paddle attachment until it's light and smooth, about 1 minute. Add the confectioners' sugar, and beat until the mixture is light and fluffy, 1 to 2 minutes.

Whisk the egg whites by hand in a medium bowl until they're foamy; then beat them into the butter-and-sugar mixture a little at a time until the're incorporated. Beat in the vanilla and lemon zest. Add the flour and salt, and beat just until smooth.

Pipe or spread 1½-inch lines of batter on the baking sheets, 2 inches apart. Let them rest at room temperature for 20 minutes.

Bake until the edges of the cookies are golden, about 10 to 12 minutes, rotating the pans once halfway through baking. Let the cookies cool on cooling racks until they harden, about 10 minutes.

Apricot Jam Half-Moons

Mezzelune di Marmellata di Albicocche

Makes about 3 dozen

1¾ cups all-purpose flour,
plus more for rolling

2 tablespoons sugar,
plus more for sprinkling

½ teaspoon kosher salt

12 tablespoons unsalted butter,
cold, cut into small pieces

1 egg, lightly beaten

2 tablespoons ice water,
or as needed

¾ cup chunky apricot jam

Heavy cream, for brushing

This is one of those simple butter-based cookies; every culture has one. They last a few weeks in a cookie tin and can be filled with any chunky jam you like. Apricot jam happens to be my favorite, but every fruit of the season had a matching jam in Nonna Rosa's cupboard, so when I was growing up the cookies varied with the seasons.

Combine the flour, sugar, and salt in a food processor, and pulse to combine. Add the butter, and pulse until the pieces are the size of small peas. Whisk the egg with 2 tablespoons of ice water, and add this to the processor. Pulse just until the dough comes together in a crumbly ball. (If the dough is still very sandy, add more water, a tablespoon at a time.)

Put the crumbly dough on the counter, and knead briefly to bring it together. Form it into a disk, wrap it in plastic wrap, and chill until it's just firm, about 1 hour.

Preheat the oven to 375 degrees. Line a baking sheet with parchment. Dust your work surface with flour, and roll the dough about ¼ inch thick. Use a 3-inch round cutter to cut out as many circles as you can. Dollop about a teaspoon of jam on one half of each circle, and brush the perimeter with cream. Fold in half, and press a fork around the edges to crimp and seal the cookie, making a semicircle. Place them on the baking sheet. Reroll the remaining dough once, to cut more circles. Use a paring knife to cut a small slit in the top of each cookie, to allow steam to vent. Brush all of the cookies with cream, and then sprinkle them with sugar.

Bake until the cookies are crisp and golden brown, about 20 to 25 minutes. Transfer them to a rack to cool. Serve them warm or at room temperature.

Rum Raisin Semifreddo

Semifreddo al Malaga

Serves 8

½ cup raisins

½ cup dark rum

4 large eggs, separated

⅔ cup superfine sugar

⅓ cup vin santo

2 teaspoons pure vanilla extract

1 cup heavy cream, chilled

1½ cups amaretti cookie crumbs

"Semifreddo" means "half cold," and refers to a kind of Italian ice cream that is not churned and never freezes hard, but instead always remains soft and creamy. I love the soft, smooth texture of this cool dessert. It is easy to assemble and put in a loaf pan, and then to form and invert out of the pan and cut into slices. But be aware that you need to serve it quickly. It can be made in almost any flavor-and-fruit combination, but this is one of my favorites. As tempted as you might be to tip that bottle of vin santo a bit more, keep in mind that it will not freeze if you overpour. But by all means, when serving the semifreddo, give yourself a glass on the side.

Line a 9-by-5-by-3 inch loaf pan with plastic wrap to overhang the edges by several inches. Put the raisins in a small bowl, and pour the rum over them. Let them soak for 15 minutes. Drain them, and reserve the rum.

Set a large heatproof bowl over barely simmering water to make a double boiler. Prepare a bowl with ice and water that the other bowl will fit into. Whisk the egg yolks, ½ cup of the sugar, and the vin santo in the bowl until the mixture is smooth; then set it over the simmering water, and whisk constantly until the mixture is light and fluffy and falls in thick pale-yellow ribbons back into the bowl, 5 to 6 minutes. (You can also use a handheld electric mixer, which will shorten the time a bit.) Set the bowl in the ice bath to cool, whisking to expedite the cooling process.

In another bowl, whisk the egg whites and remaining sugar to soft peaks, and whisk in the vanilla. Gently fold the egg whites into the cooled yolk mixture in two additions, taking care to keep the mixture light. In the bowl used for the egg whites, beat the cream to soft peaks; then fold this in two additions into the egg mixture. Quickly fold in the raisins.

Put the cookie crumbs in a small bowl. Moisten them with enough of the reserved rum so they stick together when pressed but aren't soggy (about 3 to 4 tablespoons).

Pat half of the crumbs in the bottom of the prepared pan. Spread half of the egg mixture over them in the pan; then top this with the remaining crumbs. Spread the remaining egg mixture over the crumbs. Smooth the surface with a spatula. Rap the pan on the counter to remove any air bubbles. Cover it with the overhanging plastic wrap, and freeze until firm, at least 8 hours.

To serve: Unwrap the pan, and pull out the semifreddo, using the plastic wrap as handles. Use a warm knife to cut it into slices.

Kaiserschmarrn

Serves 6

¼ cup raisins

⅓ cup rum

6 large eggs, separated

½ cup granulated sugar

Pinch of kosher salt

1 cup whole milk

2 teaspoons pure vanilla extract

1 teaspoon grated orange zest

1⅓ cups all-purpose flour

6 tablespoons unsalted butter, melted, cooled

1 cup apricot jam

Confectioners' sugar, for dusting

You will find this dessert while skiing in the Dolomites. Along the trails there are little restaurants, gathering places called "baite" (singular, "baita"), and most of them offer delicious, restorative après-ski food. The skiing experience in the Alps is about the snow, the slopes, and the scenery, but it is just as much about the food. I am no great skier, but I know that my family plan their route according to the baita they will reach for lunch or a snack. The baite do not offer chips, hamburgers, or frankfurters. Instead, local chefs cook the traditional winter fare of the mountains. This rendition of Kaiserschmarrn is one of the favorite baita treats of my grandchildren Lorenzo and Julia. It is a fluffy, light, eggy pancake topped with jam—perfect to warm a cold skier.

Put the raisins in a small bowl, and pour the rum over them. Let them soak while you make the pancake. Preheat the oven to 400 degrees.

Whisk the egg whites in a stand mixer fitted with the whisk attachment on medium speed until they're foamy. Increase the speed to high, and stream in 6 tablespoons of the sugar. Whisk them to form soft peaks, about 2 minutes. Set them aside.

In a large bowl, whisk the egg yolks with a pinch of salt to break them up. Whisk in the milk, vanilla, and orange zest until the mixture is smooth. Whisk in the flour just until it's smooth. Whisk in 3 tablespoons of the melted butter. Fold in about a third of the egg whites with a rubber spatula to lighten the batter; then fold in the remaining whites, taking care to keep the batter light by not overmixing.

Heat a large nonstick ovenproof skillet over medium heat. Brush with a little of the remaining melted butter. Pour in the batter. Drain the raisins, reserving any excess rum, and scatter the raisins over the top of the batter. Cook until the edges begin to set, 2 to 3 minutes; then bake until they're puffed and golden and a tester comes out clean, 15 to 17 minutes.

Transfer the skillet to the stovetop over medium heat. Use a big offset spatula to cut or break the pancake into cubes. Flip them to loosen them up; then drizzle them with the remaining melted butter and sugar. Cook and toss until the edges of the cubes are caramelized and golden, 3 to 4 minutes.

Warm the jam with the reserved rum in a small skillet over low heat, and stir this to combine. Divide the Kaiserschmarrn among serving plates, dust them with confectioners' sugar, drizzle with the jam sauce, and serve.

Chocolate Ricotta Brick Cake

Torta a Forma di Mattone al Cioccolato e Ricotta

Serves 8

10 ounces semisweet chocolate, chopped

1¼ pounds good-quality fresh ricotta

¼ cup superfine sugar

2 teaspoons pure vanilla extract

½ cup heavy cream, chilled

¾ cup raspberry jam

24 savoiardi

When I was a child, ricotta had many uses in the kitchen, from appetizers to pasta to stuffings to baked desserts, but I remember especially loving it for breakfast, as a snack, or for lunch, spread on a slice of country bread and drizzled with honey or just sprinkled with cane sugar. A slice of this cake makes for the perfect breakfast, to my mind, and of course makes a dessert that is just as great and easy. Ricotta is delicious cooked or uncooked, as in this dessert, where the sweet creamy cheese mixes with an assemblage of other flavors.

Line a 9-by-5-by-3-inch loaf pan with plastic wrap to overhang the sides. Melt the chocolate in a heatproof bowl set over simmering water (a double boiler). Let the chocolate cool until it's not hot to the touch but is still warm.

Combine the ricotta, sugar, and vanilla in a large bowl, and whisk well until the mixture is smooth. In another large bowl, whip the cream to soft peaks. Fold the cooled chocolate into the ricotta mixture, and then fold in the cream in two additions, keeping it light.

Put the jam in a bowl, and stir to loosen it up and make it spreadable (if it's very thick, you can add a tablespoon or two of warm water). Spread a third of the ricotta mixture in the loaf pan, and top with a single layer of savoiardi. Drizzle with half of the jam. Spread with another third of the ricotta mixture, another layer of savoiardi, and the remaining jam. Top with the remaining ricotta mixture, and top with the remaining savoiardi. Rap the pan on the counter a few times to settle it and get rid of air pockets. Cover the top loosely with plastic wrap, and refrigerate until set, at least 4 hours, though overnight is best. Unmold it, using the plastic wrap as handles, and cut into thick slices crosswise to serve.

Chocolate Cherry Panettone

Panettone con Amarene e Cioccolato

Makes 2 panettone

4 cups all-purpose flour

2 packets instant yeast
(4½ teaspoons)

Vegetable oil, for the bowl

4 large eggs

10 tablespoons unsalted
butter, cut into pieces

½ cup sugar

¾ teaspoon kosher salt

2 teaspoons pure vanilla extract

¼ teaspoon almond extract

¾ cup drained amarena
cherries, coarsely chopped

¾ cup semisweet or bittersweet
chocolate chunks

Panettone is an announcement of the Christmas holidays in Italy, although we eat it year-round: in the morning with coffee, or as a dessert topped with chocolate sauce, whipped cream, zabaglione, or a mound of ice cream. My mother, Erminia, ate more panettone than I could possibly imagine, and my daughter, Tanya, is following suit. My mother really loved it and my daughter continues to do so. They preferred this homemade version to store-bought. Panettone seems to have its origins in Milano around the eighteenth century. It evolved from bread making, enriched with butter, eggs, spices, and dried or candied fruits. In this recipe, I have combined amarena cherries and chocolate, one of my favorite dessert combinations. The uniqueness of panettone is in its rising, so make sure you give yours time to rise fully, as directed in the recipe. You'll need two 1½-quart paper panettone molds for this recipe. They're available at specialty baking shops around the holidays, or online.

The night before you want to bake, combine 1½ cups of the flour, ½ cup room-temperature water, and a pinch of the yeast in a large bowl. Mix well to combine. Oil another large bowl, add the dough, and turn it to coat in the oil. Cover it with plastic wrap, and let it sit at room temperature until bubbly, 8 to 12 hours.

Combine the dough with the remaining 2½ cups flour, the remaining yeast, ¼ cup water, 3 eggs, the butter, sugar, salt, vanilla, and almond extract in the bowl of a stand mixer. Knead on medium speed until the dough comes together in a wet ball (it won't totally clear the sides of the bowl), 5 to 6 minutes. Transfer this dough back to the oiled bowl, and let it rise until it's just starting to puff, about 1 hour.

Flatten the dough on your counter to make about an 8-inch square, and sprinkle it with the cherries and chocolate. Fold the dough over itself and knead it, to incorporate the cherries and chocolate. Form the dough into two balls, and roll your hands under the dough to make each a tight, smooth ball. Place them in two paper panettone molds (about 1½-quart →

← capacity each), cover, and let rise until they are almost doubled, about 2 hours.

Preheat the oven to 375 degrees. Beat the remaining egg, and brush the panettone with it. Bake until deep golden and cooked through (about 190 degrees inside), about 35 minutes. Cool on a rack.

Chocolate Amaretti

Amaretti al Cioccolato

Makes 2 to 2½ dozen

14 ounces almond paste

½ cup sugar

⅓ cup natural cocoa powder

¼ teaspoon kosher salt

2 large egg whites

1 teaspoon pure vanilla extract

1 cup chopped skinned hazelnuts

Amaretti cookies are chewy and delicious and naturally gluten-free, since only almond paste is used. They are holiday-and-celebration cookies all over Italy. The name "amaretti" stems from the word *amaro* ("bitter"), because they are traditionally made from bitter almonds or apricot kernels. They can be baked to a hard and crispy texture, or be soft or chewy (hence the wide range of baking times in this recipe), and can be plain or topped with pine nuts or sugar crystals. I love the flavor combination of chocolate and hazelnuts, and I incorporated it into this recipe.

They keep well in a cookie tin for a week or more.

Preheat the oven to 350 degrees. Line two baking sheets with parchment.

Break the almond paste into pieces in a food processor, and pulse them to fine crumbles. Add the sugar, cocoa, and salt. Pulse until the mixture is sandy. With the processor running, add the egg whites one at a time, and process to make a smooth, sticky dough. Add the vanilla, and pulse to incorporate. Spread the hazelnuts on a small plate.

Using a small ice-cream scoop, scoop out 1 heaping tablespoon of dough. With wet hands, roll it into a ball, and press the top into the nuts. Repeat with the remaining dough, placing the balls an inch or so apart on the baking sheets. Bake until they're puffed and just set, 16 to 18 minutes for chewy cookies, or 19 to 22 minutes for crisp ones. Remove them to a cooling rack, and cool completely.

Roasted Cranberries and Pears over Ice Cream

Pere e Cranberries al Forno con Gelato

Serves 6 to 8

1 cup orange juice

½ cup apricot jam

½ cup dry white wine

½ cup sugar

¼ cup freshly squeezed lemon juice, plus 3 strips of peel removed from the lemon with a vegetable peeler

1 vanilla bean

2 cups fresh cranberries

4 firm but ripe Bosc pears, peel left on, quartered, cored

Vanilla ice cream, for serving

Warm roasted fruits over cold ice cream is my favorite dessert, and so easy to make. I use cranberries and pears here, but you can use whatever fruits are in season—apples in fall, or peaches or other stone fruits in the summer—and berries or pitted cherries could be substituted for the cranberries. Baked fruit is my go-to dessert when I am entertaining family or friends. It can be baked ahead of time, kept warm, and then served without much hassle. It is also good for those who are watching their sugar intake. Choose your jam to complement the fruits accordingly as well.

Preheat the oven to 400 degrees.

Combine the orange juice, jam, wine, sugar, lemon juice, and peel in a 9-by-13-inch ceramic or metal baking dish, and stir to combine. Split the vanilla bean, scrape the seeds into the mixture, and add the pod. Stir in the cranberries. Nestle the pears in the sauce.

Bake until the pears are tender and the liquid is thick and syrupy, about 40 minutes. Remove the baking dish from the oven, and let it stand for about 10 minutes. (If the sauce is still too liquidy, you can return the pan to the bottom part of the oven for another 5 or 10 minutes, or transfer the sauce to a skillet to reduce it on the stovetop.) Remove and discard the lemon peel and the vanilla bean. Serve it while still warm, over ice cream.

Mimosa Cake

Torta Mimosa

Serves 8 to 10

FOR THE SPONGE CAKE

Unsalted butter, for the cake pan

1 cup all-purpose flour,
plus more for the cake pan

6 tablespoons cornstarch

6 large eggs, at room temperature

¾ cup granulated sugar

Pinch of salt

Grated zest of ½ lemon

FOR THE CUSTARD

2 cups whole milk

2 large eggs, plus 2 large egg yolks

½ cup granulated sugar

1 tablespoon cornstarch

Grated zest of ½ lemon

½ teaspoon pure vanilla extract

FOR THE SYRUP

½ cup orange juice

⅓ cup granulated sugar

2 tablespoons limoncello

FOR THE WHIPPED CREAM

1 cup heavy cream, chilled

3 tablespoons confectioners' sugar

½ teaspoon pure vanilla extract

Confectioners' sugar,
for dusting (optional)

The mimosa is a beautiful early-spring flower made up of little yellow puffballs on a branch. It is the flower that is gifted to the women in Italy for Woman's Day, La Festa della Donna, which is celebrated on March 8. Along with the mimosa flowers, the mimosa cake—a delicious light cake soaked with delightful citrus flavors—is the gift to bring or bake. I like the light airiness of the cake. I also like the beautiful blooming mimosa flowers, and that the cake celebrates women in Italy.

For the sponge cake: Preheat the oven to 325 degrees.

Butter and flour two 8-inch cake pans, and line them with parchment. Sift the 1 cup flour and the cornstarch together onto a piece of parchment.

Combine the eggs and sugar in the bowl of a stand mixer fitted with the whisk attachment. Beat on high until it's very thick (if you lift up some of the mixture with a spatula, you will be able to make a figure-8 ribbon that falls back into the batter), 7 to 8 minutes. Beat in the salt and lemon zest until everything is combined.

Remove the bowl from the mixer, and gently fold in the flour mixture in two additions. Pour the batter into the prepared pans, and bake until the cakes are light and a tester comes out clean, about 18 minutes. Let them cool for 10 minutes; then remove them from the pan and let them cool completely. Split the cooled cakes in half horizontally. With a serrated knife, cut one layer into ¼-inch cubes and set these aside on a baking sheet. Set the other three layers aside for layering.

For the custard: Put the milk in a medium saucepan, and bring it just to a boil. Remove it from the heat. Whisk the eggs, yolks, sugar, and cornstarch in a large bowl until the mixture is light and airy. Whisk in the milk a little at a time to temper the mixture. Return it to the saucepan, and set the pan over low heat. Cook, stirring constantly, until a few small steamy bubbles appear on the surface and the custard thickens, 2 to 3 minutes. Transfer it to a medium bowl, and whisk in the lemon zest and vanilla. Let it cool slightly, cover the top with →

← plastic wrap, and let it cool completely. Refrigerate until the custard is cold, about 2 hours.

For the syrup: Combine ½ cup water, the orange juice, and the sugar in a small saucepan. Simmer this over low heat just until the sugar dissolves. Remove it from the heat, and stir in the limoncello. Let it cool completely.

When you are ready to assemble, line an 8-inch springform pan with plastic wrap to overhang the edges by 3 or 4 inches.

To make the whipped cream: Whisk the heavy cream in a stand mixer until it's foamy. Add the confectioners' sugar, and whip just until it forms firm peaks. Whisk in the vanilla. Reserve ½ cup of the custard, and return it to the refrigerator. Fold a third of the whipped cream into the remaining custard to lighten it; then fold in the remaining cream until it's just combined.

Line the pan with a layer of the sponge. Brush with some of the syrup, and spread in half of the whipped cream/custard mixture. Top with another sponge layer, and gently press the sponge down all around. Brush this layer with more syrup. Spread with another half of the whipped cream/custard and the final layer of sponge cake, gently press the sponge down all around (use the top layer for this), and brush with more syrup. Fold the plastic wrap over the cake, and refrigerate until it's firm—at least 2 to 3 hours, but overnight is best. Refrigerate the remaining custard and syrup. Let the cake cubes sit on the counter, uncovered, to dry out a bit.

Remove the cake from the springform pan. Use a large spatula to remove it from the base and plastic wrap, and transfer it to a cake stand. Brush it with any remaining syrup, and spread the reserved custard over the whole cake and sides in a smooth layer. Put the reserved cake cubes on the custard on all sides of the cake, press gently to adhere them, and fill any empty spaces. Dust the cake lightly with confectioners' sugar before serving, if desired.

Acknowledgments

To write a cookbook takes an enormous team of people working together, sharing a vision for creating something that readers will enjoy, learn from, and cherish. I am very fortunate to have fantastic people by my side helping me accomplish this goal. Moments of collaboration and inspiration with all the members of the group have helped make this cookbook. It is with everyone's input—to add a pinch more of something in a recipe, or to shoot a photo from a different angle, or even to make a last-minute addition inspired by a story or memory—that this cookbook came into being. I appreciate everyone on my team so very much, and enjoy working with them. I am thankful for their enthusiasm, hard work, and energy.

This book could not have happened without Amy Stevenson, who organizes the recipe-testing process so that we are a well-oiled cooking team in the kitchen. Her expertise in recipe writing captures my flavors in the written word as we test recipes together. She gets it all down on the page perfectly, so cooks can easily follow along. It is always a pleasure to work with you, Amy—thank you. Chopping, prepping, and keeping the cooking going, Jessica Palace—your hard work is an important part of what makes this book, and I so enjoyed working with you.

Nothing happens without the team at Knopf, who have believed in me for more than twenty years and sixteen cookbooks. Peter Gethers and Tom Pold . . . thank you. Thank you for the guidance, for making this a better book, for always pushing forward and not only believing in what I do but also really enjoying it. I appreciate that. Thank you to the promotional team at Knopf, Sara Eagle and Sarah New, for getting the word out there about my books. You make it all look so easy, and I really value the incredible amount of effort you put in. Thank you, Kristen Bearse, Anna Knighton, and Kelly Blair for making my cookbook beautiful. As always, the design elements are superb, and your artistic eyes bring it all together into one tasty package!

What good would the recipes be without the mouth-watering photos full of artistry you have so skillfully taken . . . Armando Rafael. You capture my love of food through your lens. I can taste the flavors when I look at your gorgeous pictures. Thank you for paying such close attention, and for loving my food as much as I do. Grace Walker, thank you for attention to detail during photography. It is always a pleasure to work with you both.

Thank you to the American Public Television team for the fabulous work done in the distribution of my public-television series, and to Laurie Donnelly, Salme Lopez, Bara Levin, and Jeffrey Elias at WGBH. We have done some great work together over the years, and I appreciate all the effort and hard work you have put in. I would also like to thank the underwriters of my series, who help me continue to be able to share recipes with my viewers and readers: Cento, Consorzio del Grana Padano, Rovagnati Gran Biscotto, Auricchio Provolone, Locatelli Pecorino Romano, Fabbri, and Olitalia.

Thank you to my team at Tavola Productions, who make the production of my public television series possible. There are so many of you, but a special shout-out to Erika Heymann, Brittany Turk, Hayden5, Amy Stevenson, Michelli Kanuer, and their teams. I also want to thank Anthony Ventolora and the editors (Merilay Fernandez, A. J. Schultz, and Frank Bologna) for their amazing post-production work.

A special thanks to my son-in-law, Corrado Manuali, who works endlessly on the funding for the show.

And, of course, a final thank you to Olivia, Lorenzo, Miles, Ethan, and Julia . . . my shining stars.

It is important to relish the pleasure that good food and eating brings. It is not only nourishment of the body, but also of the mind and soul. My recipes are meant to be easily attainable. I want everyone to feel successful in the kitchen, and also to know they have the freedom to adapt my recipes to meet their own preferences and needs. If you pay attention to salt, use less. If you don't like spinach, substitute kale. Take liberties with my recipes to please yourself and whoever you may be cooking for.

Index

(Page references in *italics* refer to illustrations.)

A

Alette di Pollo al Formaggio al Forno (Cheesy Baked Chicken Wings), 167

Amaretti, Chocolate, *194*, 195

Amaretti al Cioccolato (Chocolate Amaretti), *194*, 195

Anchovies, Fennel with Olives and, 63

anolini, 50

    fresh pasta for, 97–8

    pasta shapes for, 99

appetizers, 3–24

    Artichokes Braised with Parsley and Prosciutto Cotto (*Carciofi con Prezzemolo e Prosciutto Cotto*), 9–10

    Baked Fresh Sardines (*Sardine al Forno*), 148

    Belgian Endive Gratin (*Indivia Belga Gratinata*), 20

    Eggplant Rollatini (*Rollatini di Melanzane*), *22*, 23–4

    Focaccia di Recco, 14–15

    Kale and Mushroom Frittata (*Frittata di Cavolo Nero e Funghi*), 17

    Leek and Ricotta Tart (*Crostata di Porri e Ricotta*), 11–13, *12*

    Prosciutto and Onion Frittata (*Frittata di Prosciutto e Cipolla*), 16

    Spicy Crispy Roasted Cauliflower (*Cavolfiore Croccante al Forno*), 18, *19*

    Vegetable Polpette (*Polpette di Verdura*), 21

    see also salads

apple(s):

    Cider-Roasted, 78

    Shredded Beet and Carrot Salad with, 34

Apricot Jam Half-Moons (*Mezzelune di Marmellata di Albicocche*), 185

Artichokes, Chicken Rollatini with Fontina and, 172

Artichokes Braised with Parsley and Prosciutto Cotto (*Carciofi con Prezzemolo e Prosciutto Cotto*), 9–10

Arugula, Ricotta Cavatelli with, 106–7

Asparagus with Lemon Sauce (*Asparagi con Salsa al Limone*), *61*, 62

Avocado, Kale Salad with Pistachios and, 36, *37*

Avocado and Tomato Salad with Balsamic and Mozzarella (*Insalata di Avocado e Pomodori con Aceto Balsamico e Mozzarella*), 32

B

Bacon, Fettuccine with Caramelized Onions, Olives and, 121

Baked Fresh Sardines (*Sardine al Forno*), 148

Barley Risotto with Cabbage and Sausage (*Risotto di Farro con Verza e Salsiccia*), 96

bean(s):

    Cannellini, Butternut Squash and, 68, *69*

    Cannellini, Warm Escarole Salad with Mackerel and, 35

    and Corn Soup with Kielbasa, *48*, 49

    and Farro Soup with Mushrooms, 52

    Fava, Soup, Cream of, with Rice, 45

    Fava, with Mint, *80*, 81

    see also chickpea(s)

beef:

    Goulash, 162, *163*

    Mixed Meat Broth, 50

Beef Rollatini (*Rollatini di Manzo*), 164–5

Beet, Shredded, Carrot and, Salad with Apple, 34

Belgian Endive Gratin (*Indivia Belga Gratinata*), 20

Braised Cabbage with Onion and Garlic (*Verza Stufata con Cipolla e Aglio*), 75

Breakfast Pasta Frittata (*Frittata di Pasta per Colazione*), 129

Broccoli Walnut Pesto, Bucatini with, 116

Brodo di Carne Mista (Mixed Meat Broth), 50

Broth, Mixed Meat, 50

Bucatini with Broccoli Walnut Pesto (*Bucatini al Pesto di Broccoli e Noci*), 116

Butternut Squash and Cannellini Beans (*Zucca con Fagioli Cannellini*), 68, *69*

C

cabbage:
Barley Risotto with Sausage and, 96
Braised, with Onion and Garlic, 75
Red, Salad with Cubed Crispy Ham, 40, *41*

cakes:
Chocolate Ricotta Brick (*Torta a Forma di Mattone al Cioccolato e Ricotta*), 190
Mimosa (*Torta Mimosa*), 197–9, *198*

calamari:
Seafood Salad, *138*, 139
Stuffed, in Tomato Sauce, 133–4

Calamari Ripieni in Sugo di Pomodoro (Stuffed Calamari in Tomato Sauce), 133–4

cannellini beans:
Butternut Squash and, 68, *69*
Warm Escarole Salad with Mackerel and, 35

Carciofi con Prezzemolo e Prosciutto Cotto (Artichokes Braised with Parsley and Prosciutto Cotto), 9–10

carrot(s):
Crispy Baked Zucchini, Cherry Tomatoes and, 67
Roasted Celery, Onions and, 74
Shredded Beet and, Salad with Apple, 34

"Cat Tongue" Cookies (*Lingue di Gatto*), 184

Cauliflower, Spicy Crispy Roasted, 18, *19*

Cavatelli, Ricotta, with Arugula, 106–7

Cavatelli di Ricotta con la Rucola (Ricotta Cavatelli with Arugula), 106–7

Cavolfiore Croccante al Forno (Spicy Crispy Roasted Cauliflower), 18, *19*

Ceci al Rosmarino (Rosemary Chickpeas), 66

Celery, Roasted Carrots, Onions and, 74

Celery Salad with Gorgonzola and Chickpeas (*Insalata di Sedano con Gorgonzola e Ceci*), 29

Cernia all'Acqua Pazza (Grouper in Crazy Water), 147

cheese:
Belgian Endive Gratin, 20
Focaccia di Recco, 14
Fontina, Chicken Rollatini with Artichokes and, 172
Four-, Baked Macaroni, 128
Gorgonzola, Celery Salad with Chickpeas and, 29
Gorgonzola, Sweet Potato Chickpea Gnocchi with, 110–11
Mozzarella, Avocado and Tomato Salad with Balsamic and, 32
Onion and Potato Gratin, 71
Zucchini Soup with Eggs and, 53

Cheesy Baked Chicken Wings (*Alette di Pollo al Formaggio al Forno*), 167

Cherry Chocolate Panettone, 191–2, *193*

chicken:
Lidia's Simple Roast, 169–70, *171*
Mixed Meat Broth, 50
Ragù, Fuzi with, 100–1
Rollatini with Fontina and Artichokes, 172
Scaloppine with Prosciutto and Peas, 168
Wings, Cheesy Baked, 167

Chicken Rollatini with Fontina and Artichokes (*Rollatini di Pollo con Fontina e Carciofi*), 172

Chicken Scaloppine with Prosciutto and Peas (*Scaloppine di Pollo con Prosciutto e Piselli*), 168

chickpea(s):
Celery Salad with Gorgonzola and, 29
Rosemary, 66
Sweet Potato Gnocchi with Gorgonzola, 110–11

Chocolate Amaretti (*Amaretti al Cioccolato*), *194*, 195

Chocolate Cherry Panettone (*Panettone con Amarene e Cioccolato*), 191–2, *193*

Chocolate Ricotta Brick Cake (*Torta a Forma di Mattone al Cioccolato e Ricotta*), 190

Chopped Frisée Salad with Salami and Boiled Eggs (*Insalata Riccia con Salame e Uova Sode*), *38*, 39

Cider-Roasted Apples (*Mele Arrosto al Sidro*), 78

Cipolla e Patate Gratinate (Onion and Potato Gratin), 71

citrus, in Mimosa Cake, 197–9, *198*

clams:
Manila, Triestina, *144*, 145
Tomato Soup with Fregola and, *54*, 55

Coniglio in Salsa di Pomodoro con Peperoni
(Rabbit in Tomato Sauce with
Peppers), 153
cookies:
Apricot Jam Half-Moons (*Mezzelune
di Marmellata di Albicocche*), 185
"Cat Tongue" (*Lingue di Gatto*), 184
Chocolate Amaretti (*Amaretti al
Cioccolato*), *194*, 195
in Strawberry and Cream Parfaits,
182, 183
Corn, Grilled Zucchini, Tomato and,
Salad, *30*, 31
Corn and Bean Soup with Kielbasa
(*Zuppa di Bobici e Fagioli con
Salsiccia Kielbasa*), *48*, 49
Corn and Greens with Prosciutto
Cotto (*Mais e Verdure con Prosciutto
Cotto*), 70
Cosciotto d'Agnello Arrosto Disossato
(Roast Boneless Leg of Lamb), *158*,
159
*Costolette di Maiale con Funghi e
Peperoni Sottaceto* (Pork Chops
with Mushrooms and Pickled
Peperoncini), 154, *155*
*Costolette di Maiale Piccanti all'Aceto con
Patate* (Spicy Vinegar Ribs and
Potatoes), 157
Cranberries, Roasted Pears and, over
Ice Cream, 196
Cream of Fava Soup with Rice
(*Vellutata di Fave con Riso*), 45
crescenza cheese, in Focaccia di
Recco, 14
Crespelle, 86
with Herb Pesto (*Crespelle con Pesto di
Erbe*), 87
Manicotti with Spinach (*Manicotti di
Crespelle con Spinaci*), 88, 89

Crispy Baked Zucchini, Carrots,
and Cherry Tomatoes (*Zucchine
Croccanti al Forno con Carote e
Pomodorini*), 67
Crostata di Porri e Ricotta (Leek and
Ricotta Tart), 11–13, *12*
Cuttlefish Salad with Potatoes and
Olives (*Insalata di Seppia con Patate
e Olive*), 142, *143*

D

desserts, 177–99
Apricot Jam Half-Moons (*Mezzelune
di Marmellata di Albicocche*), 185
"Cat Tongue" Cookies (*Lingue di
Gatto*), 184
Chocolate Amaretti (*Amaretti al
Cioccolato*), *194*, 195
Chocolate Cherry Panettone
(*Panettone con Amarene e Cioccolato*),
191–2, *193*
Chocolate Ricotta Brick Cake (*Torta
a Forma di Mattone al Cioccolato e
Ricotta*), 190
Kaiserschmarrn, 188–9
Mimosa Cake (*Torta Mimosa*), 197–9,
198
Roasted Cranberries and Pears over
Ice Cream (*Pere e Cranberries al
Forno con Gelato*), 196
Rum Raisin Semifreddo (*Semifreddo
al Malaga*), 186–7
St. Joseph's Zeppole (*Zeppole di San
Giuseppe*), 180–1
Strawberry and Cream Parfaits
(*Parfait di Fragola e Crema*), *182*, 183

E

Eggplant, Stewed Peppers and, *64*, 65
Eggplant Rollatini (*Rollatini di
Melanzane*), 22, 23–4

eggs:
Boiled, Chopped Frisée Salad with
Salami and, *38*, 39
Zucchini Soup with Cheese and, 53
see also frittatas
escarole, in Mushroom Ragù with
Greens over Polenta, 90–1
Escarole Salad, Warm, with Cannellini
Beans and Mackerel, 35

F

Farina Gnocchi (*Gnocchetti di Gris*), 56
Farro and Bean Soup with Mushrooms
(*Zuppa di Fagioli e Farro*), 52
Fava Bean Soup, Cream of, with
Rice, 45
Fava Beans with Mint (*Fave con la
Menta*), *80*, 81
Fegato alla Veneziana (Liver Venetian-
Style), 161
Fennel with Anchovies and Olives
(*Finocchio con Acciughe e Olive*), 63
Fettuccine with Caramelized Onions,
Bacon, and Olives (*Fettuccine con
Cipolle, Pancetta e Olive*), 121
Fillet of Sole in Lemon Sauce (*Filetto
di Sogliola al Limone*), 136, *137*
Finocchio con Acciughe e Olive
(Fennel with Anchovies and
Olives), 63
fish and shellfish entrees, 131–48
Baked Fresh Sardines (*Sardine al
Forno*), 148
Cuttlefish Salad with Potatoes and
Olives (*Insalata di Seppia con Patate
e Olive*), 142, *143*
Fillet of Sole in Lemon Sauce (*Filetto
di Sogliola al Limone*), 136, *137*
Grouper in Crazy Water (*Cernia
all'Acqua Pazza*), 147

fish and shellfish entrees *(continued)*

Halibut Baked in Parchment Paper (*Ippoglosso al Cartoccio*), 140

Manila Clams Triestina (*Vongole Veraci alla Triestina*), *144*, 145

Marinated Monkfish Medallions (*Medaglioni di Rospo in Saor*), 141

Mussels in Red Sauce with Linguine (*Linguine con Cozze e Pomodoro*), 146

Seafood Salad (*Insalata di Mare*), *138*, 139

Stuffed Calamari in Tomato Sauce (*Calamari Ripieni in Sugo di Pomodoro*), 133–4

Turbot Woodsman-Style (*Rombo alla Boscaiola*), 135

Focaccia di Recco, 14–15

Fontina:

Belgian Endive Gratin, 20

Chicken Rollatini with Artichokes and, 172

Four-Cheese Baked Macaroni, 128

Onion and Potato Gratin, 71

Four-Cheese Baked Macaroni (*Pasta al Forno ai Quattro Formaggi*), 128

Fregola, Tomato Soup with Clams and, *54*, 55

Fresh Pasta for Pappardelle/Tagliatelle/ Quadrucci/Fuzi/Pasutice/Anolini (*Pasta Fresca per Pappardelle/ Tagliatelle/Quadrucci/Fuzi/Pasutice/ Anolini*), 97–8

Frisée Salad, Chopped, with Salami and Boiled Eggs, *38*, 39

frittatas:

Breakfast Pasta (*Frittata di Pasta per Colazione*), 129

Kale and Mushroom (*Frittata di Cavolo Nero e Funghi*), 17

Prosciutto and Onion (*Frittata di Prosciutto e Cipolla*), 16

fuzi:

fresh pasta for, 97–8

pasta shapes for, 99

Fuzi with Chicken Ragù (*Fuzi con Sugo di Pollo*), 100–1

G

Gnocchetti di Gris (Farina Gnocchi), 56

gnocchi:

Farina, 56

small semolina, adding to Mixed Meat Broth, 50

Sweet Potato Chickpea, with Gorgonzola, 110–11

Gnocchi with Sauce from Erice (*Gnocchi con Salsa di Erice*), 108–9

Gorgonzola:

Celery Salad with Chickpeas and, 29

Sweet Potato Chickpea Gnocchi with, 110–11

Goulash, 162, *163*

Grana Padano:

Eggplant Rollatini, *22*, 23–4

Four-Cheese Baked, Macaroni, 128

gratins:

Belgian Endive, 20

Onion and Potato, 71

Green Bean, Tuna, and Potato Salad (*Insalata di Fagiolini, Tonno e Patate*), 33

greens:

and Corn with Prosciutto Cotto, 70

Mixed, Sausages with, 156

Mushroom Ragù with, over Polenta, 90–1

Grilled Corn, Zucchini, and Tomato Salad (*Insalata di Mais alla Griglia, Zucchine e Pomodori*), *30*, 31

Grouper in Crazy Water (*Cernia all'Acqua Pazza*), 147

H

Half-Moons, Apricot Jam, 185

Halibut Baked in Parchment Paper (*Ippoglosso al Cartoccio*), 140

Ham, Cubed Crispy, Red Cabbage Salad with, 40, *41*

hazelnuts, in Chocolate Amaretti, *194*, 195

I

Ice Cream, Roasted Cranberries and Pears over, 196

Indivia Belga Gratinata (Belgian Endive Gratin), 20

Insalata di Avocado e Pomodori con Aceto Balsamico e Mozzarella (Avocado and Tomato Salad with Balsamic and Mozzarella), 32

Insalata di Barbabietole, Carote e Mele (Shredded Beet and Carrot Salad with Apple), 34

Insalata di Cavolo Cappuccio Rosso con Cubetti di Prosciutto Cotto Croccante (Red Cabbage Salad with Cubed Crispy Ham), 40, *41*

Insalata di Cavolo Nero con Avocado e Pistacchi (Kale Salad with Avocado and Pistachios), 36, *37*

Insalata di Cipolle Arrosto (Roasted Onion Salad), 79

Insalata di Fagiolini, Tonno e Patate (Green Bean, Tuna, and Potato Salad), 33

Insalata di Mais alla Griglia, Zucchine e Pomodori (Grilled Corn, Zucchini, and Tomato Salad), *30*, 31
Insalata di Mare (Seafood Salad), *138*, 139
Insalata di Sedano con Gorgonzola e Ceci (Celery Salad with Gorgonzola and Chickpeas), 29
Insalata di Seppia con Patate e Olive (Cuttlefish Salad with Potatoes and Olives), 142, *143*
Insalata Riccia con Salame e Uova Sode (Chopped Frisée Salad with Salami and Boiled Eggs), *38*, 39
Insalata Tiepida di Scarola con Fagioli Cannellini e Sgombro (Warm Escarole Salad with Cannellini Beans and Mackerel), 35
Ippoglosso al Cartoccio (Halibut Baked in Parchment Paper), 140
Istria, Istrian cooking, 33, 52, 62, 145, 148
    Corn and Bean Soup with Kielbasa (*Zuppa di Bobici e Fagioli con Salsiccia Kielbasa*), 48, 49
    Goulash, 162, *163*
    Marinated Monkfish Medallions (*Medaglioni di Rospo in Saor*), 141
    Pasutice with Mixed Seafood (*Pasutice all'Istriana con Pesce*), *102*, 103

K

Kaiserschmarrn, 188–9
kale:
    Corn and Greens with Prosciutto Cotto, 70
    Sausages with Mixed Greens, 156
Kale and Mushroom Frittata (*Frittata di Cavolo Nero e Funghi*), 17

Kale Salad with Avocado and Pistachios (*Insalata di Cavolo Nero con Avocado e Pistacchi*), 36, *37*
Kielbasa, Corn and Bean Soup with, 48, 49

L

Lamb, Roast Boneless Leg of, *158*, 159
Lamb Stew with Peas (*Spezzatino d'Agnello con Piselli*), 160
Leek and Ricotta Tart (*Crostata di Porri e Ricotta*), 11–13, *12*
Lemon Cream Sauce, Spaghetti in, 115
Lidia's Simple Roast Chicken (*Pollo Arrosto alla Lidia*), 169–70, *171*
Lingue di Gatto ("Cat Tongue" Cookies), 184
linguine:
    Mussels in Red Sauce with, 146
    Spicy Lobster, 117–19, *118*
Liver Venetian-Style (*Fegato alla Veneziana*), 161
Lobster Linguine, Spicy, 117–19, *118*

M

Macaroni, Four-Cheese Baked, 128
Mackerel, Warm Escarole Salad with Cannellini Beans and, 35
Mais e Verdure con Prosciutto Cotto (Corn and Greens with Prosciutto Cotto), 70
Manicotti di Crespelle con Spinaci (Crespelle Manicotti with Spinach), 88, 89
Manila Clams Triestina (*Vongole Veraci alla Triestina*), *144*, 145

Marinara, 7
Marinated Monkfish Medallions (*Medaglioni di Rospo in Saor*), 141
mascarpone, in Strawberry and Cream Parfaits, *182*, 183
meat:
    Mixed, Broth, 50
    Shredded, Salad, 51
    see also beef; chicken; pork; sausage(s); turkey
meat and poultry entrees, 151–75
    Beef Rollatini (*Rollatini di Manzo*), 164–5
    Cheesy Baked Chicken Wings (*Alette di Pollo al Formaggio al Forno*), 167
    Chicken Rollatini with Fontina and Artichokes (*Rollatini di Pollo con Fontina e Carciofi*), 172
    Chicken Scaloppine with Prosciutto and Peas (*Scaloppine di Pollo con Prosciutto e Piselli*), 168
    Goulash, 162, *163*
    Lamb Stew with Peas (*Spezzatino d'Agnello con Piselli*), 160
    Lidia's Simple Roast Chicken (*Pollo Arrosto alla Lidia*), 169–70, *171*
    Liver Venetian-Style (*Fegato alla Veneziana*), 161
    Pork Chops with Mushrooms and Pickled Peperoncini (*Costolette di Maiale con Funghi e Peperoni Sottaceto*), 154, *155*
    Rabbit in Tomato Sauce with Peppers (*Coniglio in Salsa di Pomodoro con Peperoni*), 153
    Roast Boneless Leg of Lamb (*Cosciotto d'Agnello Arrosto Disossato*), *158*, 159

meat and poultry entrees *(continued)*
    Roast Pork Shoulder *(Spalla di Maiale Arrosto con Sidro di Mele, Sedano e Cipolle)*, 174–5
    Sausages with Mixed Greens *(Salsicce con Verdure Miste)*, 156
    Spicy Vinegar Ribs and Potatoes *(Costolette di Maiale Piccanti all'Aceto con Patate)*, 157
    Turkey Stuffed Peppers *(Peperoni Ripieni di Tacchino)*, 173
Meatballs, Turkey, Rigatoni with, 123, *124*
Medaglioni di Rospo in Saor (Marinated Monkfish Medallions), 141
Melanzane e Peperoni Stufati (Stewed Eggplant and Peppers), *64, 65*
Mele Arrosto al Sidro (Cider-Roasted Apples), 78
Mezzelune di Marmellata di Albicocche (Apricot Jam Half-Moons), 185
Mimosa Cake *(Torta Mimosa)*, 197–9, *198*
Minestra di Ricotta (Ricotta Soup), 57
Minestra di Zucchine con Uova e Formaggio (Zucchini Soup with Eggs and Cheese), 53
Mint, Fava Beans with, *80*, 81
Mixed Meat Broth *(Brodo di Carne Mista)*, 50
Monkfish Medallions, Marinated, 141
Mozzarella, Avocado and Tomato Salad with Balsamic and, 32
mozzarella, in Eggplant Rollatini, *22*, 23–4
mushroom(s):
    Farro and Bean Soup with, 52
    and Kale Frittata, 17
    Penne Rigate with Sausage, Ricotta and, 122

    Pork Chops with Pickled Peperoncini and, 154, *155*
Mushroom Ragù with Greens over Polenta *(Polenta con Ragu di Funghi e Verdure)*, 90–1
Mussel Bruschetta *(Bruschetta con Cozze)*, 8
mussels:
    Istrian Pasutice with Mixed Seafood, *102*, 103
    Seafood Salad, *138*, 139
Mussels in Red Sauce with Linguine *(Linguine con Cozze e Pomodoro)*, 146

O
olives:
    Cuttlefish Salad with Potatoes and, 142, *143*
    Fennel with Anchovies and, 63
    Fettuccine with Caramelized Onions, Bacon and, 121
onion(s):
    Caramelized, Fettuccine with Bacon, Olives and, 121
    and Potato Gratin, 71
    and Prosciutto Frittata, 16
    Roasted, Salad, 79
    Roasted Celery, Carrots and, 74
Onion and Potato Gratin *(Cipolla e Patate Gratinate)*, 71

P
Panettone, Chocolate Cherry, 191–2, *193*
Panettone con Amarene e Cioccolato (Chocolate Cherry Panettone), 191–2, *193*
Panzerotti, *5*, 6
pappardelle:
    fresh pasta for, 97–8
    pasta shapes for, 99

Pappardelle with Lamb Ragù *(Pappardelle al Ragu d'Agnello)*, 104–5
Parchment Paper, Halibut Baked in, 140
Parfait di Fragola e Crema (Strawberry and Cream Parfaits), *182*, 183
Parfaits, Strawberry and Cream, *182*, 183
pasta, 83
    adding to Mixed Meat Broth, 50
    Fresh, for Pappardelle/Tagliatelle/Quadrucci/Fuzi/Pasutice/Anolini, 97–8
Pasta al Forno ai Quattro Formaggi (Four-Cheese Baked Macaroni), 128
Pasta and Pea Soup *(Pasta e Bisi)*, 46, *47*
pasta dishes:
    Breakfast Pasta Frittata *(Frittata di Pasta per Colazione)*, 129
    Bucatini with Broccoli Walnut Pesto *(Bucatini al Pesto di Broccoli e Noci)*, 116
    Fettuccine with Caramelized Onions, Bacon, and Olives *(Fettuccine con Cipolle, Pancetta e Olive)*, 121
    Four-Cheese Baked Macaroni *(Pasta al Forno ai Quattro Formaggi)*, 128
    Fuzi with Chicken Ragù *(Fuzi con Sugo di Pollo)*, 100–1
    Istrian Pasutice with Mixed Seafood *(Pasutice all'Istriana con Pesce)*, *102*, 103
    Pappardelle with Lamb Ragù *(Pappardelle al Ragu d'Agnello)*, 104–5
    Penne Rigate with Sausage, Mushrooms, and Ricotta *(Penne Rigate con Salsiccia, Funghi e Ricotta)*, 122

Ricotta Cavatelli with Arugula (*Cavatelli di Ricotta con la Rucola*), 106–7

Rigatoni with Sausage and Cabbage (*Rigatoni con Salsiccia e Verza*), 125

Rigatoni with Turkey Meatballs (*Rigatoni con Polpette di Tacchino*), 123, *124*

Spaghetti in Lemon Cream Sauce (*Spaghetti al Limone*), 115

Spaghetti with Mixed Spring Vegetables (*Spaghetti Primavera*), 120

Spaghetti with Roasted Cherry Tomato Sauce (*Spaghetti con Pomodorini al Forno*), 126, *127*

Spicy Lobster Linguine (*Linguine all'Aragosta con Sugo Piccante*), 117–19, *118*

Timballo with Sausage Ragù (*Timballo al Ragu di Salsicce*), 112–14, *113*

see also Crespelle; gnocchi

Pasta e Bisi (Pasta and Pea Soup), 46, *47*

Pasta Fresca per Pappardelle/Tagliatelle/ Quadrucci/Fuzi/Pasutice/Anolini (Fresh Pasta for Pappardelle/ Tagliatelle/ Quadrucci/Fuzi/ Pasutice/Anolini), 97–8

Pastry Cream, 180

pasutice:

 fresh pasta for, 97–8

 Istrian, with Mixed Seafood, *102*, 103

 pasta shapes for, 99

Pasutice all'Istriana con Pesce (Istrian Pasutice with Mixed Seafood), *102*, 103

Patate Schiacciate con Aglio e Rosmarino (Smashed Garlic Rosemary Potatoes), *72*, 73

Pears, Roasted Cranberries and, over Ice Cream, 196

peas:

 Chicken Scaloppine with Prosciutto and, 168

 Lamb Stew with, 160

Penne Rigate with Sausage, Mushrooms, and Ricotta (*Penne Rigate con Salsiccia, Funghi e Ricotta*), 122

Peperoni Ripieni di Tacchino (Turkey Stuffed Peppers), 173

peppers:

 Pickled Peperoncini, Pork Chops with Mushrooms and, 154, *155*

 Rabbit in Tomato Sauce with, 153

 Stewed Eggplant and, *64*, 65

 Turkey Stuffed, 173

Pere e Cranberries al Forno con Gelato (Roasted Cranberries and Pears over Ice Cream), 196

Pesto, Broccoli Walnut, Bucatini with, 116

Pickled Peperoncini, Pork Chops with Mushrooms and, 154, *155*

Pistachios, Kale Salad with Avocado and, 36, *37*

polenta, 83

 Mushroom Ragù with Greens over, 90–1

Pollo Arrosto alla Lidia (Lidia's Simple Roast Chicken), 169–70, *171*

Polpette di Verdura (Vegetable Polpette), 21

pork:

 Bacon, Fettuccine with Caramelized Onions, Olives and, 121

 Chops with Mushrooms and Pickled Peperoncini, 154, *155*

 Ham, Cubed Crispy, Red Cabbage Salad with, 40, *41*

 Ribs, Spicy Vinegar Potatoes and, 157

 Roast, Shoulder, 174 5

 see also sausage(s)

Pork Chops with Mushrooms and Pickled Peperoncini (*Costolette di Maiale con Funghi e Peperoni Sottaceto*), 154, *155*

potato(es):

 Cuttlefish Salad with Olives and, 142, *143*

 Green Bean, and Tuna Salad, 33

 and Onion Gratin, 71

 Smashed Garlic Rosemary, *72*, 73

 Spicy Vinegar Ribs and, 157

 Vegetable Polpette, 21

Prosciutto, Chicken Scaloppine with Peas and, 168

Prosciutto and Onion Frittata (*Frittata di Prosciutto e Cipolla*), 16

prosciutto cotto:

 Artichokes Braised with Parsley and, 9–10

 Corn and Greens with, 70

provola:

 Beef Rollatini, 164–5

 Four-Cheese Baked Macaroni, 128

Pumpkin Risotto (*Risotto di Zucca*), 93

Q

quadrucci, 50

 fresh pasta for, 97–8

 pasta shapes for, 99

R

Rabbit in Tomato Sauce with Peppers (*Coniglio in Salsa di Pomodoro con Peperoni*), 153
ragù:
    Chicken, Fuzi with, 100–1
    Mushroom, with Greens over Polenta, 90–1
    Sausage, Timballo with, 112–14, *113*
raisin(s):
    Kaiserschmarrn, 188–9
    Rum Semifreddo, 186–7
Recco, Focaccia di, 14
Red Cabbage Salad with Cubed Crispy Ham (*Insalata di Cavolo Cappuccio Rosso con Cubetti di Prosciutto Cotto Croccante*), 40, *41*
Ribs, Spicy Vinegar, and Potatoes, 157
rice:
    adding to Mixed Meat Broth, 50
    Cream of Fava Soup with, 45
    see also risottos
ricotta:
    Cavatelli with Arugula, 106–7
    Chocolate Brick Cake, 190
    Eggplant Rollatini, *22*, 23–4
    and Leek Tart, 11–13, *12*
    Penne Rigate with Sausage, Mushrooms and, 122
    Soup, 57
Ricotta Cavatelli with Arugula (*Cavatelli di Ricotta con la Rucola*), 106–7
Ricotta Soup (*Minestra di Ricotta*), 57
Rigatoni with Sausage and Cabbage (*Rigatoni con Salsiccia e Verza*), 125
Rigatoni with Turkey Meatballs (*Rigatoni con Polpette di Tacchino*), 123, *124*

risottos, 92–6
    with Asparagus and Favas (*Risotto con Asparagi e Fave*), 92
    Barley, with Cabbage and Sausage (*Risotto di Farro con Verza e Salsiccia*), 96
    Pumpkin (*Risotto di Zucca*), 93
    Shrimp and Tomato (*Risotto di Gamberi e Pomodoro*), 94, *95*
Roast Boneless Leg of Lamb (*Cosciotto d'Agnello Arrosto Disossato*), 158, *159*
Roasted Celery, Carrots, and Onions (*Sedano, Carote e Cipolla Arrosto*), 74
Roasted Cranberries and Pears over Ice Cream (*Pere e Cranberries al Forno con Gelato*), 196
Roasted Onion Salad (*Insalata di Cipolle Arrosto*), 79
Roasted Spaghetti Squash with Spicy Tomato Sauce (*Spaghetti di Zucca con Salsa al Pomodoro Piccante*), 76, 77
Roast Pork Shoulder (*Spalla di Maiale Arrosto con Sidro di Mele, Sedano e Cipolle*), 174–5
rollatini:
    Beef, 164–5
    Chicken, with Fontina and Artichokes, 172
    Eggplant, *22*, 23–4
Rombo alla Boscaiola (Turbot Woodsman-Style), 135
Rosemary Chickpeas (*Ceci al Rosmarino*), 66
rum, in Kaiserschmarrn, 188–9
Rum Raisin Semifreddo (*Semifreddo al Malaga*), 186–7

S

St. Joseph's Zeppole (*Zeppole di San Giuseppe*), 180–1
salads, 27–41
    Avocado and Tomato, with Balsamic and Mozzarella (*Insalata di Avocado e Pomodori con Aceto Balsamico e Mozzarella*), 32
    Celery, with Gorgonzola and Chickpeas (*Insalata di Sedano con Gorgonzola e Ceci*), 29
    Chopped Frisée, with Salami and Boiled Eggs (*Insalata Riccia con Salame e Uova Sode*), 38, *39*
    Green Bean, Tuna, and Potato (*Insalata di Fagiolini, Tonno e Patate*), 33
    Grilled Corn, Zucchini, and Tomato (*Insalata di Mais alla Griglia, Zucchine e Pomodori*), *30*, 31
    Kale, with Avocado and Pistachios (*Insalata di Cavolo Nero con Avocado e Pistacchi*), 36, *37*
    Red Cabbage, with Cubed Crispy Ham (*Insalata di Cavolo Cappuccio Rosso con Cubetti di Prosciutto Cotto Croccante*), 40, *41*
    Roasted Onion (*Insalata di Cipolle Arrosto*), 79
    Seafood (*Insalata di Mare*), 138, 139
    Shredded Beet and Carrot, with Apple (*Insalata di Barbabietole, Carote e Mele*), 34
    Shredded Meat, 51
    Warm Escarole, with Cannellini Beans and Mackerel (*Insalata Tiepida di Scarola con Fagioli Cannellini e Sgombro*), 35

Salami, Chopped Frisée Salad with Boiled Eggs and, *38*, 39

Salsicce con Verdure Miste (Sausages with Mixed Greens), 156

Sardine al Forno (Baked Fresh Sardines), 148

Sardines, Baked Fresh, 148

sauces:
  Broccoli Walnut Pesto, 116
  Lemon, 62
  Lemon Cream, 115
  Marinara, 7
  see also ragù; tomato sauce

sausage(s):
  Barley Risotto with Cabbage and, 96
  Breakfast Pasta Frittata, 129
  Kielbasa, Corn and Bean Soup with, *48*, 49
  with Mixed Greens, 156
  Penne Rigate with Mushrooms, Ricotta and, 122
  Ragù, Timballo with, 112–14, *113*
  Rigatoni with Cabbage and, 125

Sausages with Mixed Greens (*Salsicce con Verdure Miste*), 156

scallops, sea, in Istrian Pasutice with Mixed Seafood, *102*, 103

Scaloppine di Pollo con Prosciutto e Piselli (Chicken Scaloppine with Prosciutto and Peas), 168

seafood:
  Clams, Tomato Soup with Fregola and, *54*, 55
  Lobster Linguine, Spicy, 117–19, *118*
  Mixed, Istrian Pasutice with, *102*, 103
  Mussel Bruschetta, 8
  Mussels in Red Sauce with Linguine, 146
  Salad, *138*, 139

Shrimp and Tomato Risotto, 94, *95*

see also fish and shellfish entrees

Seafood Salad (*Insalata di Mare*), *138*, 139

Sedano, Carote e Cipolla Arrosto (Roasted Celery, Carrots, and Onions), 74

Semifreddo, Rum Raisin, 186–7

Semifreddo al Malaga (Rum Raisin Semifreddo), 186–7

shellfish, *see* fish and shellfish entrees; seafood

Shredded Beet and Carrot Salad with Apple (*Insalata di Barbabietole, Carote e Mele*), 34

Shredded Meat Salad, 51

shrimp:
  Istrian Pasutice with Mixed Seafood, *102*, 103
  Seafood Salad, *138*, 139

Shrimp and Tomato Risotto (*Risotto di Gamberi e Pomodoro*), 94, *95*

Smashed Garlic Rosemary Potatoes (*Patate Schiacciate con Aglio e Rosmarino*), *72*, 73

Sole, Fillet of, in Lemon Sauce, 136, *137*

soups, 43–57
  Corn and Bean, with Kielbasa (*Zuppa di Bobici e Fagioli con Salsiccia Kielbasa*), *48*, 49
  Cream of Fava, with Rice (*Vellutata di Fave con Riso*), 45
  Farina Gnocchi (*Gnocchetti di Gris*), 56
  Farro and Bean, with Mushrooms (*Zuppa di Fagioli e Farro*), 52
  Mixed Meat Broth (*Brodo di Carne Mista*), 50
  Pasta and Pea (*Pasta e Bisi*), 46, *47*
  Ricotta (*Minestra di Ricotta*), 57

Tomato, with Fregola and Clams (*Zuppa di Pomodoro con Fregola e Vongole*), *54*, 55

Zucchini, with Eggs and Cheese (*Minestra di Zucchine con Uova e Formaggio*), 53

spaghetti:
  in Lemon Cream Sauce (*Spaghetti al Limone*), 115
  with Mixed Spring Vegetables (*Spaghetti Primavera*), 120
  with Roasted Cherry Tomato Sauce (*Spaghetti con Pomodorini al Forno*), 126, *127*

Spaghetti di Zucca con Salsa al Pomodoro Piccante (Roasted Spaghetti Squash with Spicy Tomato Sauce), 76, *77*

Spaghetti Squash, Roasted, with Spicy Tomato Sauce, 76, *77*

Spalla di Maiale Arrosto con Sidro di Mele, Sedano e Cipolle (Roast Pork Shoulder), 174–5

Spezzatino d'Agnello con Piselli (Lamb Stew with Peas), 160

Spicy Crispy Roasted Cauliflower (*Cavolfiore Croccante al Forno*), 18, *19*

Spicy Lobster Linguine (*Linguine all'Aragosta con Sugo Piccante*), 117–19, *118*

Spicy Vinegar Ribs and Potatoes (*Costolette di Maiale Piccanti all'Aceto con Patate*), 157

spinach:
  Corn and Greens with Prosciutto Cotto, 70
  Crespelle Manicotti with, *88*, 89
  Sausages with Mixed Greens, 156

Spring Vegetables, Mixed, Spaghetti with, 120

squash:
  Butternut, and Cannellini Beans, 68, *69*
  Pumpkin Risotto, 93
  Spaghetti, Roasted, with Spicy Tomato Sauce, 76, *77*
  see also zucchini
Stewed Eggplant and Peppers (*Melanzane e Peperoni Stufati*), *64*, *65*
stews:
  Goulash, 162, *163*
  Lamb, with Peas, 160
stracchino cheese, in Focaccia di Recco, 14
Strawberry and Cream Parfaits (*Parfait di Fragola e Crema*), *182*, 183
Stuffed Calamari in Tomato Sauce (*Calamari Ripieni in Sugo di Pomodoro*), 133–4
Sweet Potato Chickpea Gnocchi with Gorgonzola (*Gnocchi di Patate Dolci e Ceci al Gorgonzola*), 110–11
Swiss chard, in Corn and Greens with Prosciutto Cotto, 70

T

tagliatelle:
  fresh pasta for, 97–8
  pasta shapes for, 99
Taleggio, in Four-Cheese Baked Macaroni, 128
Tart, Leek and Ricotta, 11–13, *12*
Timballo with Sausage Ragù (*Timballo al Ragu di Salsicce*), 112–14, *113*
tomato(es):
  and Avocado Salad with Balsamic and Mozzarella, 32
  Cherry, Crispy Baked Zucchini, Carrots and, 67

Grilled Corn, Zucchini and, Salad, *30*, 31
and Shrimp Risotto, 94, *95*
Soup with Fregola and Clams, *54*, 55
tomato sauce:
  Marinara, 7
  Rabbit with Peppers in, 153
  Roasted Cherry, Spaghetti with, 126, *127*
  Spicy, Roasted Spaghetti Squash with, 76, *77*
  Stuffed Calamari in, 133–4
Tomato Soup with Fregola and Clams (*Zuppa di Pomodoro con Fregola e Vongole*), *54*, 55
Torta a Forma di Mattone al Cioccolato e Ricotta (Chocolate Ricotta Brick Cake), 190
Torta Mimosa (Mimosa Cake), 197–9, *198*
Trieste, Trieste-style cooking, xi–xii, 89
  Manila Clams Triestina (*Vongole Veraci alla Triestina*), *144*, 145
Tuna, Green Bean, and Potato Salad, 33
Turbot Woodsman-Style (*Rombo alla Boscaiola*), 135
turkey:
  Meatballs, Rigatoni with, 123, *124*
  Mixed Meat Broth, 50
Turkey Stuffed Peppers (*Peperoni Ripieni di Tacchino*), 173

V

veal, in Mixed Meat Broth, 50
Vegetable Polpette (*Polpette di Verdura*), 21
vegetables and side dishes, 58–81
  Asparagus with Lemon Sauce (*Asparagi con Salsa al Limone*), *61*, 62

Braised Cabbage with Onion and Garlic (*Verza Stufata con Cipolla e Aglio*), 75
Butternut Squash and Cannellini Beans (*Zucca con Fagioli Cannellini*), 68, *69*
Cider-Roasted Apples (*Mele Arrosto al Sidro*), 78
Corn and Greens with Prosciutto Cotto (*Mais e Verdure con Prosciutto Cotto*), 70
Crispy Baked Zucchini, Carrots, and Cherry Tomatoes (*Zucchine Croccanti al Forno con Carote e Pomodorini*), 67
Fava Beans with Mint (*Fave con la Menta*), *80*, 81
Fennel with Anchovies and Olives (*Finocchio con Acciughe e Olive*), 63
Onion and Potato Gratin (*Cipolla e Patate Gratinate*), 71
Roasted Celery, Carrots, and Onions (*Sedano, Carote e Cipolla Arrosto*), 74
Roasted Onion Salad (*Insalata di Cipolle Arrosto*), 79
Roasted Spaghetti Squash with Spicy Tomato Sauce (*Spaghetti di Zucca con Salsa al Pomodoro Piccante*), 76, *77*
Rosemary Chickpeas (*Ceci al Rosmarino*), 66
Smashed Garlic Rosemary Potatoes (*Patate Schiacciate con Aglio e Rosmarino*), 72, 73
Stewed Eggplant and Peppers (*Melanzane e Peperoni Stufati*), *64*, 65
Vellutata di Fave con Riso (Cream of Fava Soup with Rice), 45

Venetian-style cooking:
  Baked Fresh Sardines, 148
  Liver, 161
Verza Stufata con Cipolla e Aglio
  (Braised Cabbage with Onion and
  Garlic), 75
Vinegar Ribs and Potatoes, Spicy, 157
Vongole Veraci alla Triestina (Manila
  Clams Triestina), *144*, 145

W

Walnut Broccoli Pesto, Bucatini with,
  116
Warm Escarole Salad with Cannellini
  Beans and Mackerel (*Insalata
  Tiepida di Scarola con Fagioli
  Cannellini e Sgombro*), 35
Woodsman-Style Turbot, 135

Z

Zeppole, St. Joseph's,
  180–1
Zeppole di San Giuseppe (St. Joseph's
  Zeppole), 180–1
Zucca con Fagioli Cannellini (Butternut
  Squash and Cannellini Beans),
  68, *69*
*Zucchine Croccanti al Forno con Carote
  e Pomodorini* (Crispy Baked
  Zucchini, Carrots, and Cherry
  Tomatoes), 67
zucchini:
  Crispy Baked Carrots, Cherry
    Tomatoes and, 67
  Grilled Corn, Tomato and, Salad,
    30, 31
  Vegetable Polpette, 21

Zucchini Soup with Eggs and Cheese
  (*Minestra di Zucchine con Uova e
  Formaggio*), 53
*Zuppa di Bobici e Fagioli con
  Salsiccia Kielbasa* (Corn and
  Bean Soup with Kielbasa),
  48, 49
Zuppa di Fagioli e Farro (Farro
  and Bean Soup with
  Mushrooms), 52
Zuppa di Pomodoro con Fregola e Vongole
  (Tomato Soup with Fregola and
  Clams), *54*, 55

Me on a staircase above the Giardini di Pola in the early 1950s

LIDIA BASTIANICH, Emmy Award–winning public television host, best-selling cookbook author, restaurateur, and owner of a flourishing food-and-entertainment business, has married her two passions in life—her family and food—to create multiple culinary endeavors.

Lidia's cookbooks, coauthored with her daughter, Tanya, include *Lidia's Celebrate Like an Italian, Lidia's Commonsense Italian Cooking, Lidia's Favorite Recipes, Lidia's Italy in America, Lidia Cooks from the Heart of Italy,* and *Lidia's Italy*—all companion books to the Emmy-winning and three-time-nominated television series *Lidia's Kitchen, Lidia's Italy in America,* and *Lidia's Italy,* which have aired internationally, in Mexico, Canada, the Middle East, Croatia, and the U.K. Lidia has also published *Felidia, Lidia's Mastering the Art of Italian Cuisine, Lidia's Family Table, Lidia's Italian-American Kitchen, Lidia's Italian Table,* and *La Cucina di Lidia,* and three children's books: *Nonna Tell Me a Story: Lidia's Christmas Kitchen, Lidia's Family Kitchen: Nonna's Birthday Surprise,* and *Lidia's Egg-citing Farm Adventure,* as well as a memoir, *My American Dream.* Lidia is the chef-owner, with her son, Joseph, of Becco. She is also the founder of Tavola Productions, an entertainment company that produces high-quality broadcast productions. Lidia also has a line of dry pastas and all-natural sauces, called LIDIA'S. Along with her son, Joe Bastianich, and Oscar Farinetti, she opened Eataly, the largest artisanal Italian food-and-wine marketplaces in New York City, Chicago, Boston, Los Angeles, Las Vegas, Toronto, San Jose, Dallas, and São Paulo, Brazil.

TANYA BASTIANICH MANUALI'S visits to Italy as a child sparked her passion for the country's art and culture. She dedicated herself to the study of Italian Renaissance art during her college years at Georgetown; she then earned a master's degree from Syracuse University and a doctorate from Oxford University. She lived and studied in many regions of Italy for several years, and taught art history to American students in Florence. But it was in New York that she met her husband, Corrado Manuali, who came from Rome.

Tanya spearheads the production of Lidia's public television series, as an owner and executive producer of Tavola Productions, and is active in the restaurant business at Lidia's Kansas City, MO. Tanya joined her brother in operating several other restaurants, including Babbo, Lupa, Pizzeria Mozza, Osteria Mozza, and Chi Spacca. Joe and Tanya partnered with Tommy Mazzanti to expand and develop the famous Italian sandwich shop All'Antico Vinaio in the United States. Tanya has also led the development of the Lidia brand on social media platforms, related publications, and merchandise lines of tableware and cookware.

Together with Corrado, Tanya oversees the production and expansion of the LIDIA'S food line of all-natural pastas and sauces. Tanya has coauthored several books with her mother, including *Lidia's a Pot, a Pan, and a Bowl*; *Felidia*; *Lidia's Celebrate Like an Italian; Lidia's Mastering the Art of Italian Cuisine; Lidia's Commonsense Italian Cooking; Lidia's Favorite Recipes; Lidia's Italy; Lidia Cooks from the Heart of Italy;* and *Lidia's Italy in America*. In 2010, Tanya coauthored *Reflections of the Breast: Breast Cancer in Art Through the Ages,* a social–art-historical look at breast cancer in art from ancient Egypt to today. In 2014, Tanya wrote *Healthy Pasta* with her brother, Joe.

A NOTE ON THE TYPE

This book was set in Hoefler Text, a family of fonts designed by Jonathan Hoefler, who was born in 1970. First designed in 1991, Hoefler Text was intended as an advancement on existing desktop computer typography, including as it does an exponentially larger number of glyphs than previous fonts. In form, Hoefler Text looks to the old-style fonts of the seventeenth century, but it is wholly of its time, employing a precision and sophistication only available to the late twentieth century.

Composed by North Market Street Graphics, Lancaster, Pennsylvania

Printed and bound by C&C Offset, China

Designed by Anna B. Knighton